"I might consider adding a new salesperson because my company appears to be getting busier. But if in two months I realize that business is not in fact coming back as quickly as I had thought, and I need to lay off this person, I will likely end up paying out $5,000, $10,000, or even $20,000 in unemployment taxes for the person I hired and then laid off...the disincentives far outweigh the incentives."

–Jay Goltz, NY Times "You're the Boss".

1 Introduction

The United States is the only OECD country to finance unemployment insurance (UI) through a tax system which penalizes layoffs. The original intent of this institution, know as "experience rating," was to apportion the costs of UI to the highest turnover firms and potentially stabilize employment.[1]

Experience rating might stabilize employment through a layoff cost. The layoff cost is levied when a firm lays off a worker and is assessed a higher tax rate in the future. The cost of layoffs, therefore, reduces the incentive for a firm to shed workers. On the other hand, an increased firing burden causes firms to reduce hiring given the prospect of having to lay off workers in the future. In this paper, I study experience rating both theoretically and empirically, analyzing its effects on the dynamics of the labor market.

Due to the sharp increase in unemployment during the Great Recession, state UI trust funds are deeply in debt. Between 2007 and 2011, state trust fund reserves fell by $62 billion; in 2011, states owed $40 billion in loans to the federal government and currently still owe about $20 billion.[2] State governments are therefore grappling with new UI financing policies to cover these trust funds and ensure solvency into the future, making an evaluation of their efficacy timely. I use a general equilibrium model of experience-rated taxes to study the labor market effects of tax changes that are similar to those currently under consideration.

This paper is the first to empirically quantify the relationship between job flows and UI financing. Macroeconomists have long recognized that job flows are large compared to net employment growth, and important in shaping the evolution of labor market outcomes (See Davis et al. (2010)). This paper sheds light on the types of labor market policies that drive gross job flows and policy changes that affect employment volatility. This paper also advances the literature on the effect of microeconomic employment adjustment costs on hiring and firing.[3] While adjustment costs are often hard to directly measure, this paper analyzes a quantifiable adjustment cost and provides

---

[1] The origin of the idea for experience rating is attributed to John R. Commons who helped draft the 1932 Wisconsin bill that introduced "merit-rating."

[2] See Vroman (2011) for a summary of UI finances since the Great Recession.

[3] A comprehensive literature review is beyond the scope of this paper. See, for example, Hamermesh and Pfann (1996).

novel evidence on its effect on job flows using firm-level data.

After reviewing the relevant features of UI experience rating, I present a dynamic labor demand problem for a firm facing increasing payroll taxes as a function of its endogenously-determined, individual layoff history. One important contribution of this paper is that I model realistic UI tax schedules. In practice, states set minimum and maximum tax rates and therefore not all firms face increasing tax rates from a layoff. This induces economically important non-linearities in firm labor demand depending on its past layoff history.

Much of the previous literature has instead modeled experience rating as an exogenous linear layoff cost, for instance in Anderson (1993). In this type of linear layoff cost model, there is a "band of inaction" in which the firm does not hire or fire over a range of labor productivity realizations. The band of inaction is also present when I introduce layoff costs based on experience rating. However, in this case experience rating imposes a cost that is a function of the *stock* rather than the *flow* of layoffs, which implies that the band of inaction is a function of each firm's entire history of layoffs. Hence, I find that firm heterogeneity in layoff experience is crucial to understanding the general equilibrium effects of experience rating.

The model predicts how experience rating affects job flows. The higher is experience rating, measured as the fraction of benefits paid back in higher taxes, the lower are the rates of both job creation and job destruction. Having established that experience rating reduces both job creation and job destruction in a dynamic model of firm labor demand, I test this prediction empirically. I collect a dataset of UI tax schedules and financing rules across states between 2001-2010. With these data, I calculate the "marginal tax cost" of experience rating following, for example, Topel (1983), and Card and Levine (1994). The marginal tax cost gives the fraction of benefits charged to a firm that are paid back in future higher taxes. I combine these data with confidential firm-level data on gross job flows from the Quarterly Census of Employment and Wages (QCEW). The results show that increasing experience rating by 5% would reduce job destruction by about 2% and job creation by 1.5%.

In the next section, I embed the firm's dynamic problem in a search model of unemployment to study the effect of experience rating on the aggregate labor market. While previous work such as l'Haridon and Malherbet (2009) and Albertini (2011) has examined experience rating in a search model, the model presented is the first to study UI taxes that are endogenously determined in a heterogeneous agent, DSGE framework. I build on the model developed by Elsby and Michaels (2013) who introduce firm heterogeneity with endogenous job destruction and aggregate uncertainty in a search and matching model of unemployment. I use the idiosyncratic layoff histories across firms to match the empirical cross-sectional distribution of firms across UI tax rates.

I then present results from tax experiments in the long-run and the short-run. Because I capture more realistic features of UI tax schedules as well as heterogeneity across firms in UI tax rates, I can analyze the effect of a rich set of tax experiments which previous models could not consider. First,

I study various changes to the tax schedule that all imply an equal increase in experience rating but have different effects on the labor market. All experiments that raise experience rating reduce job creation and destruction. A 5% increase in experience rating reduces job flows between 1.1% and 1.9%. These results are quantitatively consistent with the empirical estimates, which imply a drop between 1% and 2% in job flows. The unemployment rate declines in each experiment, falling on average by .21 percentage points (a drop of 2.9%). The magnitude of the decline in the unemployment rate depends on whether the tax burden and firm profits increase or decrease.

In light of the heterogeneity in the outcomes across tax changes, I conduct two policy experiments which close about 50% of financing gap in UI trust funds. In one experiment, I raise the tax schedule uniformly across firms, a policy akin to those undertaken recently in some states. Alternatively, I raise the same amount of revenue by increasing the slope of the UI tax schedule. I find that raising experience rating instead of a uniform tax increase can actually reduce unemployment while raising the same amount of revenue.

Lastly, I solve the model with aggregate uncertainty using the approximate equilibrium method of Krusell and Smith (1998) to study the effect of experience rating on the business cycle. Model impulse responses to productivity shocks show that experience rating reduces the amplitude of the labor market response to business cycles. For instance, 10% higher experience rating reduces the unemployment rate response by .045 percentage points, amounting to a 6.8% smaller labor market slump. I also find that experience rating introduces strong non-linearities and asymmetries in the business cycle response to aggregate shocks, a feature that is notoriously hard to generate in standard search models (Barnichon (2010), Petrosky-Nadeau and Zhang (2013)). Unemployment rises more than proportionally with the aggregate shock due to the incidence of higher UI tax rates. There is also a slower recovery of unemployment as the larger stock of accumulated layoffs leads to persistently higher tax rates. With experience-rated taxes, the response of the labor market to a boom is smaller in magnitude than to a bust since firms' payroll taxes do not rise to compound the decline in productivity as it does in a recession. However, experience rating still dampens the response of the labor market after a positive productivity shock; firms know that any hiring will be undone after the shock fades, and a higher tax hit for those future layoffs will reduce vacancy posting upon impact.

The plan of the paper is as follows. Section 2 reviews the salient institutional details of UI financing. Section 3 develops a theoretical prediction for job flows and Section 4 estimates this relationship empirically. Section 5 presents a DSGE model of the labor market with realistic UI financing and Section 6 conducts policy experiments. Section 7 discusses some related literature and Section 8 concludes.

2 Experience Rating of Unemployment Insurance Taxes

Before reviewing the related literature, it is necessary to understand the basic structure of UI finance. The United States finances its unemployment insurance system through a payroll tax that increases with a firm's past layoffs. In 1938, Wisconsin introduced the first experience rating system in which each firm was independently assessed a tax rate to cover benefits drawn by its laid off workers. By 1948, all states had adopted some system of experience rating for UI financing.

In the current system, each firm pays a payroll tax on its current wage bill. For each employee, the firm pays a tax on a capped base of salary, determined by each state. In 2010, this taxable base varied from $7,000 to $36,800. Federal law mandates that employers with at least three years of experience with layoffs must be experience-rated but allows states to charge new employers a reduced rate not less than 1%.[4]

The system of experience rating, however, is "imperfect" since tax rates are capped at statutory minimum and maximum levels. Firms with no layoff risk are mandated to contribute to the pool of funds whereas firms with the highest layoff risk pay a lower rate than they would under a perfectly rated system. Across all states in 2010, the minimum rate varied from 0% to 2.2% and the maximum rate was no lower than 5.4% and reached 13.6%.[5] Thus, the finance system induces a cross-subsidy from low to high layoff firms and industries.

States generally use one of two types of experience rating. In 2010, 17 states and territories used a "benefit ratio" method and 33 states and territories used the "reserve ratio."[6] Figures 1 and 2 show examples of typical tax schedules for a reserve ratio and a benefit ratio state. In Nevada, the minimum rate charged is .25% up to a maximum rate of 5.4% with the tax rate increasing in the firm's experience factor (on the x-axis), determined by its reserve ratio. In Alabama, firms with the lowest benefit ratio (on the x-axis) are charged the minimum rate of .74% while the highest benefit ratio firms are charged the maximum rate of 7.14%.

In the benefit ratio system, each employer pays a payroll tax based on the ratio of benefits drawn by that firm's laid off workers to the size of its covered payroll over a three to five year window. The tax rate takes on a minimum value for firms with low benefit ratios and a maximum value for firms with high ratios. In a reserve ratio system, states maintain an account for each firm that is debited due to benefits drawn by its laid off workers and is credited with tax payments. The net reserve as a ratio of the firm's payroll over a three to five year period determines the payroll tax rate, again between some minimum and maximum rates. Therefore, an additional layoff reduces

---

[4]In practice, most states offer a "standard" flat rate to new employers between 1% and 6.2% for one to three years before implementing experience rating. The reduced rates in some states led to a practice known as SUTA dumping by which firms would change account numbers before eligibility for the higher experience-rated rate. Legislation in 2004 attempted to curb this practice.

[5]The minimum value of the maximum tax rate is set by a federal tax credit of 5.4% in 2010.

[6]Michigan and Pennsylvania use a combination but predominantly use the benefit ratio. Oklahoma and Delaware use a benefit wage ratio system. These four states are therefore excluded from the empirical analysis.

the firm's reserve ratio and increases the tax rate, assuming it is not at the minimum or maximum rate.

Given the complexity of UI taxes, many previous studies, such as Topel (1983), calculated the "marginal tax cost" to quantify the degree of experience rating. The marginal tax cost is defined as the present discounted value of benefits paid back in future taxes by a firm. Consider a firm on the sloped portion of the tax schedule. If that firm lays off an additional worker, the firm is charged for the benefits he or she draws, causing the tax rate to rise according to the given tax schedule. The marginal tax cost determines the fraction of those additional benefits the firm pays back in taxes. Further details of the specific financing systems and marginal tax cost formulas are given in Section 4.

3 A Theoretical Prediction for Job Flows

In this section, I establish a theoretical prediction for the effect of experience rating on job creation and job destruction to be tested empirically. I present a stripped down version of the full model presented later in order to characterize qualitatively the effect of experience rating on labor demand and job flows.

A firm maintains a stock of workers, n_{-1}, and a stock of layoffs, ℓ_{-1}. Of the laid off, a fraction δ are no longer counted on the firm's books for taxation purposes. This occurs if the laid off find other jobs or there is a statutory time limit for benefit liability. The firm observes idiosyncratic productivity x and decides to hire or fire. If it fires, it sends those workers into the pool, ℓ. Firms take the wage, w, as given and pay all workers the same rate.[7] Note that I have assumed that firms cannot recall workers from their stock of layoffs. Appendix A relaxes this assumption and shows that allowing the firm to rehire from its stock of layoffs is isomorphic to reducing the marginal cost per layoff. The stock of layoffs evolves according to the following equation of motion

$$\ell = (1-\delta)\ell_{-1} + \mathbb{1}^{-}\Delta n,$$

where $\mathbb{1}^{-}\Delta n$ is the number of layoffs if the firm is firing ($\mathbb{1}$ is used throughout as the indicator function). Tax rates are set as follows. The firm pays a payroll tax on its current employment, n, where the tax rate $\tau(\ell)$ is

$$\tau(\ell) = \begin{cases} \underline{\tau} & \text{if } \ell < \underline{\ell} \\ \tau_c \cdot \ell & \text{if } \ell \in [\underline{\ell}, \bar{\ell}] \\ \bar{\tau} & \text{if } \ell > \bar{\ell}. \end{cases}$$

The tax schedule the firm faces thus matches the salient features of realistic state UI schedules: the

---
[7]In the model developed in Section 5, I endogenize the wage.

tax rate is linearly increasing between a statutory minimum and maximum rate. Figure 3 graphs the tax schedule as a function of layoffs.

The firm's labor demand problem is to choose n to maximize profits, discounting future profits at the discount rate β, as given by the following dynamic programming problem, subject to the equation of motion for ℓ:

$$\Pi(n_{-1}, \ell_{-1}, x) = \max_n \left\{ xF(n) - wn - \tau(\ell)wn + \beta \int \Pi(n, \ell, x') dG(x'|x) \right\} \tag{1}$$

3.1 Firm policy functions

I first describe the qualitative nature of the firm's labor demand functions. Suppose ℓ is low enough such that the firm is on the flat portion of the tax schedule at the minimum rate. It could lay off workers and end up at three positions of the tax schedule: at the maximum rate (eqn. 2), the sloped portion (3), or remain at the minimum rate (4). Alternatively, it could hire and remain on the flat portion (5). The first order conditions for those possibilities are as follows

$$xF'(n) - w - w\bar{\tau} + \beta \frac{\partial}{\partial n} \int \Pi(n, \ell > \bar{\ell}, x') dG = 0 \tag{2}$$

$$xF'(n) - w - w\tau(\ell) + \beta \frac{\partial}{\partial n} \int \Pi(n, \ell \in [\underline{\ell}, \bar{\ell}], x') dG = wn\tau'(\ell) \tag{3}$$

$$xF'(n) - w - w\underline{\tau} + \beta \frac{\partial}{\partial n} \int \Pi(n, \ell < \underline{\ell}, x') dG = 0 \tag{4}$$

$$xF'(n) - w - w\underline{\tau} + \beta \frac{\partial}{\partial n} \int \Pi(n, \ell_{-1}(1-\delta) < \underline{\ell}, x') dG = 0. \tag{5}$$

The first three terms of equations (2)-(5) are simply the marginal product of labor minus the after-tax wage. The following term is the discounted marginal value of labor which depends on the choice of n and ℓ and the expectation over future productivity. The term on the right hand side of (3) represents the layoff cost imposed by experience rating on the sloped portion of the tax schedule. Before examining that more closely, I turn to equations (4) and (5).

It is important to note that the flow costs to the firm in equations (4) and (5)—the first three terms—are identical. They differ only because the continuation value depends on the future stock of layoffs. The stock of layoffs is higher if the firm lays off a worker rather than hiring a worker (or remaining at n_{-1}). Since higher layoffs lead to weakly higher payroll taxes, the forward value is weakly declining in the stock of layoffs (for a given n and x). Therefore, even away from the sloped portion of the schedule, the firm's decision is affected by the potential of increasing taxes. This highlights the importance of modeling experience-rated taxes in which the tax rate depends on the history of each firm's layoff decisions, in contrast to the previous literature, such as Anderson (1993), which has generally modeled experience rating as a linear layoff cost.

Examining equation (3) further highlights the importance of realistically modeling experience rating. Recall that this is the first order condition for a firm that begins the period at the minimum rate (i.e., $\ell_{-1} < \underline{\ell}$) but lays off enough workers so that its choice of ℓ lies on the sloped portion. Again, the first three terms on the left hand side are the marginal product of labor minus the after-tax wage. Here, the after-tax wage is increasing in the marginal layoff. On the right hand side, the layoff cost is represented by $wn\tau'(\ell)$, which is the marginal payroll tax paid on the *entire* wage bill. Therefore, the layoff cost under experience rating is crucially *not only* on the flow of layoffs, but rather a higher tax paid on *all* inframarginal workers, with the tax rate based on the entire *stock* of layoffs.

In contrast to this model, suppose instead the firm had to pay a constant linear cost of $\tau_f > 0$ for each worker it laid off. In that case the first order condition for the firm, irrespective of its previous, layoffs would be

$$xF'(n) - w + \beta \frac{\partial}{\partial n} \int \Pi(n, x') dG = -\tau_f. \qquad (6)$$

This is the standard linear adjustment cost model. In this case, the policy function would exhibit a band of inaction at n_{-1} since the first layoff is always costly. In this simpler model, however, the firm's labor demand decision is a not affected by its previous history of layoffs. The firm also does not have to consider a higher tax rate it must pay on the *entire* current stock of employed workers.

Turning to the labor demand functions in this model, it is useful to break the firm's decision into three cases (see Figure 3): Case 1 is for firms that begin the period at the minimum tax rate; Case 2 is for firms that begin on the sloped portion and Case 3 is for firms at the maximum tax rate. The policy function for Case 1 is depicted in Figure 4a, with the log of employment on the y-axis and the log of productivity on the x-axis.[8] The horizontal line gives the firm's stock of employment at the beginning of the period ($\ln(n_{-1})$). Because the firm is on the flat portion of the schedule, the firm locally hires and fires costlessly; the policy function is, therefore, linear through $\ln(n_{-1})$.[9]

The firm's marginal lay off is costless at $\ln(n_{-1})$. For a low enough $\ln(x)$, however, the firm must decide between shedding workers and incurring a tax increase or maintaining a higher workforce than otherwise would be optimal. For a range of $\ln(x)$, the profit maximizing choice is to halt layoffs to avoid the adjustment cost. Because the firm defers layoffs for a range of productivities, the policy function is flat for a range of x draws as shown in the flat "band of inaction" on the labor demand schedule in Figure 4a. At a certain point, the draw of x is low enough so that a lower employment level generates higher profits despite the higher tax rate. When an additional layoff does warrant the adjustment cost, the firm chooses a tax rate on the sloped portion of tax schedule. Since the first layoff generates a discontinuous cost due to the higher tax rate on current payroll, the firm sheds a fraction of its employment. This is evident in the steep negative slope of

---

[8] I choose the log of the firm's states since, in the frictionless model, the labor demand schedule is linear in the logs.
[9] With the addition of search costs, the firm would also have a band of inaction at n_{-1}.

the policy function at that point.

The bottom panel of this figure plots the associated tax rate that the firm optimally chooses. As described above, the firm chooses to remain at the minimum rate until a bad enough shock induces a bout of layoffs. In that case, the tax rate (at just below $\ln(x) = 0$) jumps up on to the sloped portion. As the firm lays off more workers, the tax rate continues to rise.

Figure 4b shows the policy function for Case 2 in which the firm begins the period on the sloped portion. In Case 2, the band of inaction rests at $\ln(n_{-1})$ as the marginal layoff is costly since the firm is on the sloped portion. As ℓ_{-1} increases, the policy function shifts to the right since the firm pays a higher tax rate per employee and thus holds a lower stock of employment for a given $\ln(x)$. The dashed blue line depicts a policy function for a firm that starts with a relatively higher stock of layoffs. For a low enough shock (around -.1), this firm sheds enough workers to reach the maximum tax rate. The dashed blue line shifts down as the firm reaches the maximum tax rate. Finally, the demand schedule in Case 3 (not shown) would mimic the frictionless demand schedule since the cost of an additional layoff is zero. The schedule is linear in the log of employment. Due to the positive payroll tax, however, the level of employment is lower than it would be without the tax.

3.2 Job Flows and Experience Rating

What does the model predict for job flows? For firms that face the upward-sloping tax schedule, the marginal layoff is costly, and firms defer layoffs and maintain a higher than optimal workforce. The firm would prefer to decrease its stock of employment due to lower productivity per worker, but for each layoff it pays a higher tax rate on its entire remaining workforce. As is also true in a standard layoff cost model, the firing cost also acts as a hiring cost. For any worker that is hired today, the firm will pay a layoff cost for that worker with a positive probability. Millard and Mortensen (1996) show that in a standard Mortensen-Pissarides model, linear layoff costs unambiguously reduce both job creation and job destruction. This section shows that in a model where layoff costs are determined by the entire stock of layoffs and the cost is paid on each inframarginal worker, the same is true.

I use the model of the previous section to preview the prediction for job flows by varying the degree of experience rating. Starting from the calibrated parameters of the full model of Section 5 but abstracting from search costs ($c = 0$), I vary the degree of experience rating and measure job flows.[10] In practice, I do this by varying the upper threshold of the tax schedule to increase or decrease its slope. As fully described later, I calculate a marginal tax cost for this model in a similar fashion as the empirical literature—the present discounted value of benefits paid back in

---

[10] The previous section assumed fixed wages for ease of exposition. In this simulation, I assume the bargained wage as derived in Section 5.2. The results of the simulation are robust to the wage assumption.

future taxes.[11]

Job flows are calculated from simulated data as they are in the empirical analysis following Davis and Haltiwanger (1992). They define job creation (destruction) as the gross increase (decrease) in employment at expanding (contracting) firms. The job creation (destruction) rate is gross job creation (destruction) divided by the average of the current and previous employment over all firms. Formally, let N_t be employment at time t and $X_t = .5\sum(N_t + N_{t-1})$ be the average of employment in time t and $t-1$. Then the rates of job creation and job destruction are given by

$$JC = \frac{\sum_{\Delta n>0} \Delta N_t}{X_t}, \; JD = \frac{\sum_{\Delta n<0} |\Delta N_t|}{X_t}. \tag{7}$$

Job reallocation, a measure of the total amount of job flows in the labor market, is given by $JR = JC + JD$. Net employment growth is $Net = JC - JD$. Note that in any steady state without trend growth, $\Delta N \equiv 0$ will imply $JC \equiv JD$. Therefore, the sign of the change of JR with respect to a change in the marginal tax cost gives the sign of the change in both JC and JD.

Figure 5 shows the simulated job flows plotted for a range of marginal tax costs between 15% and 78%. Job reallocation falls monotonically with marginal tax cost, going from over 16% with a marginal tax cost of 15% to under 6% with a MTC of 78%. As shown below, the slope of this line implies a 23% decrease in job flows if states implemented 100% experience rating from an empirical mean of 54%. Do firms behave as the model predicts in practice? To answer this question, I now turn to an empirical evaluation of experience rating and job flows.

4 Empirical Evaluation of Experience Rating

In this section, I exploit state and industry variation in experience rating to evaluate its effect on U.S. job flows. Unfortunately, data on UI tax contributions at the firm-level are not available to exploit state heterogeneity in tax laws. While these data would be preferable, I study differences in jobs flows across detailed industries that face varying UI tax schedules at the state level. I first compile a dataset of state UI tax provisions from the Department of Labor. For each state and year, I collect data on the minimum rate, maximum rate, and the slope of the tax schedule.[12] I combine these tax schedules with firm-level data from the Quarterly Census of Employment and Wages to estimate the relationship between experience rating and job flows. I turn first to describing the data used to analyze the effect of experience rating on job flows. I then describe how I quantify the level of experience rating across states and industries for the econometric analysis that follows.

---

[11] The equation giving the model's marginal tax cost is described fully below in Section 5.5.

[12] Primarily these data come from Section C of the 204 report collected by the DOL from state UI agencies. These data are available in a consistent format between 2001-2010.

4.1 QCEW Data

The data used to measure labor market outcomes are from the Quarterly Census of Employment and Wages (QCEW). The QCEW is a census of establishments with employment covered by UI, making it an ideal source of data for the questions at hand. The entire database covers 99.7% of wage and salary employment. Establishments in the QCEW are linked across quarters to create the Longitudinal Database of Establishments from 1990 Q2–2010 Q2.

I have been granted access by the Bureau of Labor Statistics to QCEW micro-data for 40 states, including Puerto Rico and the Virgin Islands (shown in Table A1). The remaining states are either excluded due to the legal arrangement or due to incomparable experience rating systems.[13] Establishments in the data are identified by an UI tax account number. I define a firm as an agglomeration of establishments with a common UI account number. This implicitly treats firms as single-state entities and ignores employment decisions across states that may be due to differing marginal tax costs. I return to this below.

There are several additional restrictions in the data that are worth noting. Monthly employment at the establishment is defined as employment in the pay period including the 12th of the month. Following BLS procedure, quarterly employment is defined as employment in the third month of each quarter. I also only consider firms that are continuing between quarters and therefore abstract from openings and closing.[14] In addition, I exclude from the analysis establishments within firms that engaged in a consolidation or breakout between quarters due to difficulties in correctly apportioning the employment change across quarters. These exclusions allow me to extend the QCEW back to the second quarter of 1990.[15]

Multi-establishment firms can potentially have establishments in several industries. In order to examine firm behavior by industry, I assign the industry of largest establishment to the entire firm. Finally, I exclude public sector establishments and NAICS sectors 92 and 99 from the analysis as UI finance differs in the public sector.

After applying these restrictions, I calculate statistics at the 3-digit NAICS-by-state level. This results in 3,377 3-digit NAICS-by-state cells observed for 80 quarters from 1990 Q2 to 2010 Q1. For each cell, I calculate the job creation and job destruction rates as given above in (7). Additionally, job reallocation is $JR = JC + JD$ and the net change is $JC - JD$. These variables are the primary outcomes examined in the econometric analysis below. I now describe in detail the two primary UI financing systems in order to construct a measure of experience rating across states and industries.

---

[13] Table 6 and Appendix C show a robustness check using additional data from the missing states.

[14] The effect of experience rating on openings and closing is an important extension given the concern with SUTA dumping. Estimates of firm birth and death rates on experience rating do not indicate that this is quantitatively important, however.

[15] Faberman (2008) extends the LBD back to 1990 using a careful matching algorithm to account for breakouts and consolidations.

4.2 Reserve Ratio System

The most common system of UI tax determination is the "reserve ratio" system. In reserve ratio states, firms have an account with the state from which unemployment benefits are debited and to which taxe payments are credited. Each year, the firm's reserve ratio is calculated as the ratio of its reserve balance, R_t, to the average of its payroll over the past three years. The reserve ratio is then converted into a tax rate based on the tax schedule that will be in effect for the next year.[16] Recall that taxes are paid on each employee up to a maximum taxable wage base (between \$7,000 and \$37,000).

The tax schedule in a reserve ratio state is a declining function of the reserve balance, R_t. Firms with a highly negative account balance are subject to the statutory maximum rate while firms with the most positive balances are subject to the statutory minimum rate. Between the minimum and maximum rates, firms with more negative balances are required to pay higher tax rates. A linear approximation of the tax schedule between the minimum and maximum rates is: $\tau_t = \lambda_0 - \lambda_1 r_{t-1}$, where the reserve ratio, r_t, is given by $r_t = \frac{R_t}{\bar{w}\bar{n}}$, and $\bar{w}\bar{n}$ is average taxable payroll.

Calculation of Marginal Tax Cost

Due to the unavailability of individual firm tax rates, I follow Card and Levine (1994) and calculate the marginal tax cost for an average firm in a given state and industry. Let n be the level of employment and $1 + g_n$ be the gross annual growth of employment in a given industry within a state at time t. Further, let w be the taxable wage base in that state and $1 + g_w$ be the annual growth in the taxable wage base. In the data, I estimate $(1 + g_n)$ and $(1 + g_w)$ as the average annual growth rates from 2001 Q1 to 2007 Q4, the business cycle peaks over the relevant time frame. Consider the reserve balance of an industry in a particular state on the sloped portion of the tax schedule

$$R_t = R_{t-1} + \tau_t w_t n_t - B_t, \tag{8}$$

where B_t is the dollar value of benefits charged to the industry. B_t is composed of the proportion of benefits that are charged to firms in each state, χ, and the value of benefits, b_t, paid to the those beneficiaries, $B_t = \chi b_t$.[17] The reserve ratio is the ratio of the reserve balance, R_t, and the average taxable payroll over a three year period. Due to the assumption of constant growth of n and w, average payroll over a three year period is $w_{t-1} n_{t-1}$. Converting to a reserve ratio by dividing both sides by $w_{t-1} n_{t-1}$ gives the approximate reserve ratio:

$$r_t \approx \frac{R_t}{w_{t-1} n_{t-1}} = \frac{r_{t-1}}{(1+g_n)(1+g_w)} + (1+g_n)(1+g_w)\tau_t - \frac{\chi b_t}{w_{t-1} n_{t-1}}. \tag{9}$$

---

[16] Computation dates are typically January 1st. Four states use July 1st.
[17] χ is typically less than 100% since certain types of benefits are not fully charged to firms.

If a firm is at the minimum or maximum tax rate, an addition dollar of benefits charged does not increase the tax rate, so the marginal tax cost is zero. If the industry is on the sloped portion, then the tax rate is linearly related to the reserve ratio as given by

$$r_t = \frac{\lambda_0 - \tau_{t+1}}{\lambda_1}. \tag{10}$$

Substituting for r_t and manipulating gives

$$\lambda_0(1-(1+g_n)(1+g_w))w_t n_t + \tau_t w_t n_t(1-\lambda_1(1+g_n)(1+g_w)) + \lambda_1(1+g_n)^2(1+g_w)^2\chi b_t = \tau_{t+1}w_{t+1}n_{t+1}. \tag{11}$$

The present discounted value of the firm's tax bill, discounted at the nominal interest rate i, can be written as

$$T_t = \sum_{j=0}^{\infty} \left[\frac{1}{1+i}\right]^{t+j} w_{t+j} n_{t+j} \tau_{t+j}. \tag{12}$$

The marginal tax cost is the derivative of the present discounted value of future taxes with respect to an increase in benefits. Substituting in the left hand side of equation 11 in to equation 12, we find

$$MTC = \frac{\partial T}{\partial B_t} = \frac{\chi\lambda_1(1+g_n)^2(1+g_w)^2}{i + \lambda_1(1+g_n)^2(1+g_w)^2}. \tag{13}$$

The marginal tax cost is linearly increasing in χ, the fraction of benefits charged to firms. The MTC is also decreasing in the interest rate. In a reserve ratio state, due to discounting future tax payments by the discount rate, the marginal tax cost is necessarily below 100%. In the simple case where $g_n = g_w = 0$, however, it is easy to verify that the MTC is increasing in the slope of the tax schedule if $\lambda_1 > -i$, which will be satisfied for any positive interest rate.

4.3 Benefit Ratio System

The other method of experience rating a firm's tax rate is the benefit ratio system. States charge a tax rate that is proportional to the value of benefits drawn by laid off workers divided by its payroll. The previous three to five years of benefits and payrolls are used in determining the benefit ratio.

Calculation of Marginal Tax Cost

Call T the number of years of benefits and payrolls used in the calculation. Then the benefit ratio is given by

$$BR_t = \frac{\sum_{j=1}^{T} \chi B_{t-j}}{\sum_{j=1}^{T} w_{t-j} n_{t-j}}. \tag{14}$$

Under the assumption of constant growth of employment and taxable wages as above, the benefit ratio can be approximated by

$$BR_t \approx \frac{\sum_{j=1}^{T} \chi B_{t-j}}{T\bar{w}n}$$

and the tax schedule by

$$\tau_t = \lambda_0 + \lambda_1 BR_t.$$

Multiplying both sides by $w_t n_t$, the tax bill of a firm can be written as

$$w_t n_t \tau_t = w_t n_t \lambda_0 + \lambda_1 w_t n_t \frac{\sum_{j=1}^{T} \chi B_{t-j}}{T\bar{w}n}.$$

The discounted present value of an additional dollar of benefits is

$$MTC = \chi \lambda_1 (1+g_n)^2 (1+g_w)^2 \frac{1-(1+i)^{-T}}{Ti}. \tag{15}$$

In a benefit ratio system, it is clear that the marginal tax cost can rise above 100% depending upon the slope of the tax schedule. Further, inspecting the equation shows that the marginal tax cost for a benefit ratio state is linearly increasing in the slope of the tax schedule and the fraction of benefits charged to firms. With a bit of algebra, it can be shown that the marginal tax cost is also decreasing in the discount rate.

4.4 Accounting for the minimum and maximum tax rates

The above calculations for the marginal tax cost only apply to firms on the sloped portion of the tax schedule. For firms that are on the flat portion—either assigned the minimum or maximum tax rates—the marginal tax cost of an additional layoff is approximately zero.[18] I use newly available QCEW tabulations on the overall UI tax contributions at the 3-digit industry and state cell to place an average firm in each cell on the sloped or flat portion of the tax schedule.

Using these data, I calculate for each state and industry cell the average tax rate for each quarter from 2001 forward. If the industry's tax rate is above the maximum or below the minimum, therefore, I set the marginal tax cost to zero. Requiring the average tax rate in a cell to be at the minimum or maximum is a very restrictive assumption which is infrequent in the sample. Therefore, I implement this in the following way. If an industry is ever at the minimum or maximum, I set the marginal tax cost to zero in all years. Depending on the distribution of firms across tax rates within each industry, this is a conservative method of assigning cells to the sloped portion which would tend to attenuate regression coefficients.

---

[18] As pointed out in the model above, the marginal tax cost for a firm that approaches the sloped portion is non-zero. I follow the literature and assign the marginal tax cost as zero at the minimum rate as well. Importantly, imposing this assumption biases the results against finding a significant effect of experience rating.

These newly available data on tax rates provide a significant improvement over the previous literature. In previous studies, it is commonly assumed that over a long period of time, tax contributions must equal benefits paid. Given this assumption, researchers used the average unemployment rate within each cell to determine the level of taxes required to fund those benefits in steady state. If these steady state tax rates were below the minimum or above the maximum, the marginal tax cost was set to zero.

There are several problems encountered with this method. First, as Pavosevich (2009) points out, over the time period of this study, tax contributions fell far short of benefits paid, causing large deficits in many state trust funds. Therefore, the steady state tax assumption is inappropriate in recent years. Indeed, over the recent period, the steady state tax rates implied by this method swamp the maximum tax rate in nearly all cells. Second, while a state must eventually equate contributions with benefits, it is not necessarily true that this must hold for each industry within a state, especially since persistent industial cross-subsidies are inherent in the system. Third, assigning the marginal tax cost to zero as a function of each state-by-industry unemployment rate induces a simultaneity in the dependent variable—the probability of unemployment in Card and Levine (1994)— with the calculated marginal tax cost. The method in this paper, therefore, reduces misclassification of zero marginal tax cost cells as well as avoids the simultaneity problem inherent in previous studies.

4.5 Discount Rate Calculation

In both experience rating systems, the nominal interest rate is an important parameter since previous benefits are charged to the firm in nominal terms. I apply several different values for the interest rate. First, I follow the literature and set the nominal interest rate to 10%. Second, I calculate the interest rate as the sum of a nominal interest rate on corporate paper and add to that the quarterly probability of firm closure in the QCEW micro data.[19] This discount rate varies over state and industry but is only available from the detailed micro data from the QCEW in this study. Third, as a robustness check, I use interest rates of 5% and 15% as well (see Table 4). Overall, the results with different interest rates are qualitatively similar.

4.6 Econometric Analysis

Table 1 shows summary statistics for several of the variables for the states listed in Table A1. First, the average marginal tax cost using the exogenous interest rate is 54% with a maximum of 217%. The average is somewhat lower than the 68% in Card and Levine (1994) whereas the maximum in their sample was 1.6.[20] The lower average over the recent period accords with Pavosevich (2009)

---

[19] I use the 3 month AA non-financial corporate paper rate from the FRED database (DCPN3M).
[20] Regressions omitting $MTC > 1.5$ yielded substantially similar results.

who shows that states are charging firms too little to finance their UI trust funds. Figure 6 graphs the marginal tax cost by two-digit industry. Variation within each two-digit industry is across state as well as 3-digit industries within the two-digit sector. From this graph we can see that the largest spikes at zero marginal tax cost (either from the minimum or maximum rate) are in mining, construction, and arts and entertainment. I find that retail trade is less likely to be at the maximum tax rate than is found in Card and Levine (1994).

The average marginal tax cost with the estimated interest rate is similar to that with the exogenous interest rate. The average is a 61% MTC with the same standard deviation and a slightly higher maximum value of 220%. Over the entire sample, the job destruction rate averaged 6.48 and job creation averaged 6.23 for a mean net creation rate of -.25 over the entire period. Total flows in the labor market, measured by the job reallocation rate, werexs 12.5% per quarter. I now turn to the econometric analysis of experience rating and job flows.

The baseline specification is a standard fixed effects model with the job destruction rate, job creation rate, net creation rate, or the reallocation rate as outcomes. I follow the literature and average the marginal tax cost over all of the observations within each 3-digit industry and state cell and apply that average to all quarters of data. Therefore, the variation that is exploited in this regression is the *between* variation in the level of the marginal tax cost. This requires assuming that there are fixed differences at the 3-digit industry across states as well as fixed state effects (constant across industries). The full specification is

$$Y_{isyq} = \varsigma + \varsigma_i + \varsigma_s + \varsigma_y + \varsigma_q + \beta MTC_{is} + x'_{isyq}\kappa + \epsilon_{isyq} \tag{16}$$

The ς's are fixed effects for 3-digit industry, state, year, and quarter.[21] x_{isyq} includes the level of employment and the number of firms in each cell to control for the size of the cell and κ are the associated coefficients. β is the coefficient of interest and gives the effect of going from 0% to 100% MTC on the dependent variable.

Table 2 shows results from the regression with the averaged marginal tax cost using the exogenous interest rate of 10%. The coefficient on the marginal tax cost is -2.4. This implies that a change from the mean of 54% to 100% marginal tax cost would reduce job destruction by 17%. The coefficient on job creation is -1.86. The point estimate suggests that implementing perfect experience rating would reduce job creation by 13.7%. Moreover, instituting a 100% MTC from the average of 54% would reduce job reallocation by 10%. The right panel is the same analysis conducted using on the period 2001-2010, as these are the actual years that I measure marginal tax costs. The results are qualitatively similar, but with larger coefficients for job destruction and job reallocation.

Table 3 presents estimates using two different marginal tax cost measures. The left panel shuts

---

[21]Specifications with year × quarter dummies are nearly identical.

down employment growth in the marginal tax cost calculation, i.e. $g_n = 0$.[22] In this specification, job destruction would fall by 15.8% and job creation by 15.4% after instituting 100% experience rating. As another robustness check, I calculate the marginal tax cost as in Topel (1983) which amounts to setting $g_n = g_w = 0$ and $\chi = 1$, shown in the right panel of Table 3. Note that this regression only exploits variation in the slope of the tax schedule across states. The results are much the same with a slightly larger decrease in job creation than job destruction (13.4% vs. 16.5%).

Table 4 presents estimates using alternative discount rates. The first two panels use alternative exogenous interest rates. The coefficients on the marginal tax cost in each of these regressions are significant. Using a 5% interest rate, job destruction is predicted to fall by 12.2% if perfect experience was instituted. With a 15% interest rate, job destruction would fall by 22%. Results for the other outcomes are similar to those found in Tables 2 and 3. The right-most panel uses an estimated interest rate adding the estimated death rate in the QCEW to the corporate paper rate for each quarter. I estimate this on the subsample over which I calculate the marginal tax costs from 2001-2010. The result are even stronger in this specification. Going from average to perfect experience rating would reduce job destruction by 29% while reducing job creation by 23% (both significant). Job reallocation would be reduced by about 20% and net creation is economically and statistically significantly positive.

In the next set of estimates in Table 5, I regress the job destruction and creation rates including several additional measures of the tax schedule as controls. In the left column of each panel (labeled (1)), I include the proportion of the state's accounts that are on the sloped portion of the schedule as well as its interaction with the marginal tax cost. The motivation for this is that the higher the fraction on the sloped portion, the more likely the marginal tax cost will be to bind. Therefore, we should expect a negative sign on the interaction.[23] As expected, the interaction effect is significantly negative, showing that if the slope is binding for more firms, there is a larger negative effect of increasing experience rating on job flows.[24]

Column (2) of each panel includes the proportion on the slope (not interacted) as well as the percent of benefits charged, and the minimum and maximum statutory rates. These turn out to be insignificant with the exception of the maximum rate on job destruction. The coefficient on the marginal tax cost remains large and significant. [25]

One caveat to the analysis above is the definition of the firm. Recall that I define a firm as the collection of establishments under the same UI account number, which is unique to each state's unemployment insurance system. Some firms, of course, have establishments across several states.

---

[22]I also try specifications including g_n, g_w, and χ as regressors. Results are similar.

[23]Admittedly, this suggests that the method of assigning a zero MTC as described in Section 4.4 does not fully disentangle firms on the sloped portion from the flat portions.

[24]Additionally, estimating job creation and job destruction as a system of equations yields quantitatively similar results.

[25]See Appendix C and Table 6 for an additional robustness check with missing states.

It is therefore possible that firms might shift employment to low marginal tax cost states and concentrate its turnover in that state, thereby generating a negative relationship between layoffs and the marginal tax cost. While the incentive from the firm's perspective is to avoid the layoff cost, the question remains as to whether higher experience rating in one state actually reduces overall job flows.

It is difficult to identify multi-state firms and their associated job flows in the QCEW. Instead, I focus on firms with only one establishment within each state and discard firms with multiple establishments under the same UI accounts as a sensitivity check. It is more likely that these firms only have one establishment and are not multi-state firms. The results from the baseline specification for JC and JD are shown in Table 7. Again, the results are significant and quantitatively similar—job destruction would fall by 14% and job creation by 10% if an average marginal tax cost state implemented 100% repayment.

Finally, it is possible that the anticipation of the marginal cost of a layoff affects the firm entry and exit decision. So far, the model of labor demand and the empirical work has just considered continuing firms. In principle, firm's might decide to exit the market rather than lay off a large fraction of its workforce to avoid the tax hike. Analysis of the firm birth and death rates calculated from the QCEW data do not show that this is a substantial concern. Table 8 shows the effect of the marginal tax cost on the fraction of firms that die or are born within a quarter in a 3-digit state-by-industry cell. From these regressions, it appears that experience rating does not have a large effect on the entry and exit decision as the coefficients on both the birth and death rates are small and insignificant.

The empirical evidence presented in this section strongly confirms the prediction that higher experience rating reduces the firm's incentives to both create and destroy jobs. I now turn back to a fully-specified macroeconomic model to understand the effect of experience rating on long-run and short-run aggregate labor market outcomes.

5 Macroeconomic Equilibrium and Dynamics with Tax Experiments

In this section, I develop a search model of unemployment with heterogeneous firms that face UI taxes based on endogenously-determined, individual layoff histories. I analyze this model to understand the effect of experience rating on the dynamics of the labor market and to consider counterfactual UI financing. The model is an extension of Elsby and Michaels (2013) who develop a search and matching model of the labor market with large firms and endogenous job destruction. Having large firms is essential for the question at hand, since its necessary to keep track of a non-degenerate distribution of layoff stocks, which would not be possible in a single worker-firm setting.

The economy is populated by a measure one of firms and measure $\mathbb{L}$ of workers. Aggregate productivity at a given time is p_t and follows an autoregressive process in logs: $\ln p_t = \rho_p \ln p_{t-1} + \epsilon_t^p$. Firm level idiosyncratic productivity is also assumed to follow an AR(1) process in logs: $\ln x_t = \rho_x \ln x_{t-1} + \epsilon_t^x$. Firms have access to identical production functions and workers are ex-ante homogeneous. Productivity at the firm level is merely the product of the level of each, px. Firms observe aggregate and idiosyncratic productivity and workers observe aggregate productivity and the idiosyncratic productivity of its employer or potential match.

Workers and firms meet through a process of search and matching governed by an aggregate matching function. The rates of job finding and job filling are determined by the aggregate number of vacancies, V, and the aggregate number of searchers, U. As is standard in the literature, the matching function is assumed to be constant returns to scale: $M(U,V) = M(1, \frac{V}{U})$. Define labor market tightness, $\theta \equiv \frac{V}{U}$. The higher is θ, the more job openings per searching worker and, therefore, the tighter the labor market.

Unemployed workers meet a job posting at the job finding rate, $f(\theta) \equiv \frac{M(U,V)}{U}$. The standard assumptions apply: $f'(\theta) > 0$ and $f(0) = 0$. A posted vacancy is filled at the job queueing rate, $q(\theta) \equiv \frac{M(U,V)}{V}$; $q'(\theta) < 0$ and $q(\infty) = 0$.

Unemployment insurance benefits, b, are financed through two forms of taxes. (1) firm-specific, experience-rated payroll taxes, τ, based on individual firm's history of layoffs; (2) lump sum taxes, T, on firms and all workers (whether unemployed or not). These taxes are set each period to balance the government budget constraint. Since they are equally levied and non-distortionary, they do not affect the optimal decisions of the agents. Thus, they are ignored in exposition of the model below.[26]

The timing of events in the model is as follows. At the beginning of each period, firms evaluate the idiosyncratic and aggregate state of the economy and decide to post vacancies or lay off workers. Unemployed workers meet firms and bargain over wages while laid off workers cycle into unemployment. After all job flows are complete, production occurs and wages are paid, which completes a time period.

The model's key endogenous variables are determined mainly by the labor demand decision of individual firms, to which I now turn.

5.1 Firm's Problem

The firm's labor demand problem is similar to that presented in Section 3. Recall that the firm has a stock of workers, n_{-1}, and a stock of layoffs, ℓ_{-1}. Of the laid off, a fraction δ no longer determine the firm's UI tax. Previous layoffs are no longer counted in a firm's stock if the laid off

---

[26] In reality, firms pay taxes on a capped portion of payroll. I abstract from this for simplicity.

find other jobs or there are statutory benefit-liability time limits.[27] In Section 6.3, I endogenize the depreciation rate to vary with the aggregate job finding rate, but for now keep it fixed.[28]

The firm observes idiosyncratic productivity, x, and aggregate productivity, p, and decides to hire or fire. Let the number of hires be denoted by h and the number of fires as s. As opposed to the costless hiring in Section 3, the firm must post vacancies at a cost of c per vacancy. Each vacancy meets a worker with probability q, a firm hiring h workers must post $\frac{h}{q}$ vacancies. If it fires s workers, it sends those workers into the layoff pool, ℓ. Therefore, the equations of motion for the firm's state variables are

$$n = n_{-1} + h - s$$

$$h = qv, \text{ and}$$

$$\ell = (1-\delta)\ell_{-1} + s.$$

Since $s \equiv -\mathbb{1}^{-}\Delta n > 0$, it is possible to rewrite the equation of motion for layoffs as: $\ell = (1-\delta)\ell_{-1} - \mathbb{1}^{-}\Delta n$. In addition, $h \equiv \mathbb{1}^{+}\Delta n = qv$. Total hiring costs are given by $cv \equiv \frac{c}{q}\mathbb{1}^{+}\Delta n$. The firm's optimization problem is written entirely in terms of n and Δn according to these equations.

In addition to idiosyncratic state variables, the firm must take account of several aggregate states. Along with the level of aggregate productivity, the firm must predict future queuing rates to make optimal vacancy posting decisions. In this setting, that amounts to forecasting future labor market tightness, θ'. The reason for this is fairly intuitive. Suppose that aggregate productivity was in a long drought so that many firms had shed workers. After aggregate productivity recovers, firms will be looking to hire a large number of workers and labor market tightness will be high. On the other hand, suppose that aggregate productivity had realized a series of positive shocks. Firms will have a larger than typical stock of workers; in response to the same positive shock, firms will hire fewer workers and so tightness will be relatively lower. Therefore, aggregate productivity is not sufficient for firms to determine the price of hiring, firms must also predict aggregate tightness.

In order to forecast labor market tightness, the firm must keep track of the type distribution of firms across state variables, $\{n, \ell, x\}$. Call this distribution Ξ and the transition equation $\Xi' = \Gamma(p, \Xi)$ which is a function of aggregate productivity as well. It is important to note that endogenous aggregate variables depend on aggregate productivity and the type distribution of firms: $\theta = \theta(p, \Xi)$, $f = f(\theta(p, \Xi))$, $q = q(\theta(p, \Xi))$, and $\delta = \delta(f(\theta(p, \Xi)))$. In what follows, the dependence of these

---

[27] Geometric depreciation of layoffs through δ is a parsimonious reduced-form method to model laid off workers finding new jobs without tracking their employment history. In addition, it captures the statutory maximum amount of time that previous benefits are charged to a firm. Even in reserve ratio states in which previous benefits are forever counted, previous layoffs are diminished through tax contributions over time that restore a firm's balance. It is also worth noting that δ will be integral in matching the distribution of firms across tax rates.

[28] Relative to a fixed δ, the mechanisms that cause a reduction in unemployment and dampened aggregate response are in fact strengthened when allowing δ to vary with the job finding rate.

variables on the aggregate state is suppressed. Therefore, the following is the firm's Bellman equation

$$\Pi(n_{-1}, \ell_{-1}, x, p, \Xi) = \max_{n} \left\{ pxF(n) - wn - \tau(\ell)wn - \frac{c}{q}\mathbb{1}^+ \Delta n \right.$$
$$\left. + \beta \int \int \Pi(n, \ell, x', p', \Xi') dG(x'|x) dP(p'|p) \right\} \quad (17)$$

such that

$$\ln x' = \rho_x \ln x + \epsilon^x \quad (18)$$
$$\ell = (1-\delta)\ell_{-1} - \mathbb{1}^- \Delta n \quad (19)$$
$$\mathbb{1}^+ \Delta n = qv \quad (20)$$
$$\ln p' = \rho_p \ln p + \epsilon^p \quad (21)$$
$$\Xi' = \Gamma(p, \Xi). \quad (22)$$

5.2 Wage Setting

For tractability, the workers' side of the model is kept extremely simple. In particular, I abstract from the situation in which laid off workers remain on call with their previous firm. If firms could recall (as Appendix A shows), this would give rise to an option value of remaining on recall with that firm versus searching in the general labor market. I leave this interesting extension for future research.

Workers can either be employed at a firm with n employees, ℓ laid off workers, and productivity x, or unemployed. An unemployed worker earns a flow unemployment benefit of b. Unemployed workers find a job with probability f. The Bellman equation for an unemployed worker is given by

$$W^u(p, \Xi) = b + \beta E\left[f'W^e(n', \ell', x', p', \Xi') + (1-f')W^u(p', \Xi')\right]. \quad (23)$$

An employed worker in the current period earns wage w and is fired with probability $\tilde{s}$ into the layoff pool.

$$W^e(n, \ell, x, p, \Xi) = w + \beta E\left[\tilde{s}'W^u(p', \Xi') + (1-\tilde{s}')W^e(n', \ell', x', p', \Xi')\right]. \quad (24)$$

For additional simplicity, I will assume that wages are simply the weighted average, with bargaining power η, of the average flow surplus from working and the average flow surplus from employing n workers, gross of adjustment costs.[29] [30] The flow surplus from working is just $w - b$. The average

---

[29] Several papers make this assumption such as Barlevy (2002), Shimer (2001), and others.

[30] Stole and Zwiebel (1996) bargaining is intractable in this model due to the interaction of the layoff cost and the unknown optimal employment policy function in the continuation value of the firm's problem. Numerical derivatives

flow surplus from employing n workers is

$$\frac{pxF(n) - (1+\tau(\ell))wn}{n}. \qquad (25)$$

The assumed bargain is, therefore,

$$\eta\left[\frac{pxF(n) - (1+\tau(\ell))wn}{n}\right] = (1-\eta)\left[w - b\right]. \qquad (26)$$

Solving for the wage gives

$$w = \frac{\eta \frac{pxF(n)}{n} + (1-\eta)b}{1 + \eta\tau(\ell)} = \frac{\eta pxn^{\alpha-1} + (1-\eta)b}{1 + \eta\tau(\ell)}. \qquad (27)$$

There are several important features of the wage in comparison to the standard bargained wage that should be noted. First, as is standard, conditional on labor productivity, the wage is declining in n due to diminishing marginal productivity. Second, as expected, the wage is (weakly) decreasing in the UI tax rate. In the standard model, the wage is typically a function of future labor market tightness—firms must compensate workers when the labor market is tighter as the outside of option of finding another job is easier. Therefore, the wage will co-vary with productivity substantially less without this additional term. As is well known, this will lead to substantial amplification of shocks relative to comparable models.

5.3 Aggregation and Equilibrium

Let the policy function for the firm be denoted as

$$n^* \equiv \Phi(n, \ell, x, p, \Xi), \quad \Delta_p(n, \ell, x, p, \Xi) \equiv \Phi(n, \ell, x, p, \Xi) - n. \qquad (28)$$

and

$$\ell^* = (1-\delta)\ell - \mathbb{1}^{-}\Delta_p(n, \ell, x, p, \Xi). \qquad (29)$$

where $\mathbb{1}^{\{+,-\}}$ is an indicator for positive or negative employment adjustment. Total separations are given by

$$S = \int_n \int_\ell \int_x \mathbb{1}^{-}\Delta_p(n, \ell, x, p, \Xi) d\Xi(n, \ell, x), \qquad (30)$$

Total hires are described by

---

of value functions are subject to substantial error at early stages of value function iteration. This makes numerically solving the full bargaining problem intractable.

$$H = \int_n \int_\ell \int_x \mathbb{1}^+ \Delta_p(n,\ell,x,p,\Xi) d\Xi(n,\ell,x). \tag{31}$$

Employment is simply the average employment level across firms

$$\bar{N} = \int_n \int_\ell \int_x \Phi(n,\ell,x,p,\Xi) d\Xi(n,\ell,x). \tag{32}$$

Employment evolves according to the following difference equation

$$\bar{N} = \bar{N}_{-1} + H - S. \tag{33}$$

Finally, the evolution of the aggregate stock of layoffs is

$$\bar{L} = (1-\delta)\bar{L}_{-1} - \int_n \int_\ell \int_x \left[\mathbb{1}^- \Delta_p(n,\ell,x,p,\Xi)\right] d\Xi(n,\ell,x). \tag{34}$$

These accounting rules allow me to define an equilibrium of the model.[31] A *recursive stationary equilibrium* is a set of functions

$$\{\Pi, \Phi, H, S, \bar{N}, \bar{L}, W^e, W^u, w, \theta, f, q, \delta, \bar{s}, \Gamma\}$$

such that:

1. Firm's problem: taking θ as given, firms maximize Π subject to the bargained wage, w, and the optimal choice is consistent with Φ.

2. Wage bargaining and worker flows: the wage function, w, splits the flow surplus between the worker and firm. The finding and separation rates along with the wage bargain and the value of leisure satisfy the worker's Bellman equations.

3. Hiring and separations consistent with f and $\bar{s}$:

    - Hiring, H, is consistent with Φ and $f = \frac{H}{\mathbb{L}-\bar{N}}$
    - Separations, S, are consistent with Φ and imply $\bar{s} = \frac{S}{\bar{N}}$
    - θ is given by the matching function and is consistent with f.

4. Employment Dynamics: $\bar{N} = \bar{N}_{-1} + H - S$

5. Model Consistent Dynamics: The evolution of aggregate employment and layoffs given by Γ is consistent with Φ and the processes for p and x.

---

[31] Note that the government fills any holes in UI financing through a lump sum tax that does not distort the optimal choices of any of the agents. It is therefore abstracted from here.

5.4 Solution Method

The solution to the dynamic labor demand problem stated above is analytically intractable, therefore I use to numerical methods to solve the model. The crux of the solution is to pin down the policy function for the firm, Φ. To accomplish this, I use value function iteration on the firm's recursive problem stated in equation (17).

Specific details of the algorithm are described in Appendix B. I briefly describe the computational method to solve for the steady state allocation here. First, I discretize the state space which consists of $\{n, \ell, x\}$. I discretize the shock process x using the method in Tauchen (1986). I discretize n on an equally spaced grid between one-half of the minimum frictionless employment level and two times the maximum frictionless employment level. In order to reduce computation time, I restrict the firm to choose points on the discrete grid for n.

I then discretize the grid for layoffs: the maximum of the layoff grid is chosen as the maximum employment change in the frictionless model. Since the firm chooses an employment level which pins down the layoff stock next period, I linearly interpolate at points off the layoff grid. In practice, firms in equilibrium do not reach the highest point of the layoff grid. Therefore, I use an unequally spaced grid with more points at the bottom two-thirds of the grid. Finally, in the simulations, I ensure that firms do not hit the end points of either the employment or layoff grids.

After I solve the firm's policy function, I simulate the model for 10,000 firms and 3,000 periods, discarding the first 1,000 observations as the burn-in period. I simulate the continuous shock process in logs and piece-wise linearly interpolate between points on the grid.[32] The aggregation of the simulation across all time periods and agents following equations (29)-(33) constitutes the solution to steady state equilibrium.

Approximate Aggregation

In each period, firms decide on vacancy posting given their idiosyncratic state vector and the aggregate state of the economy. In order to predict future levels of labor market tightness (and therefore vacancy posting costs), firms must forecast the entire type distribution of firms across the state space. This dependence is shown by the inclusion of Ξ in the firm's optimization problem. Since Ξ is an infinite-dimensional object, the exact equilibrium is not computable. I follow the Krusell and Smith (1998) approximate equilibrium approach.[33]

The approach is as follows. Instead of forecasting the entire distribution of firms across states, I assume the firm is boundedly rational and only keeps track of a finite set of moments of the distribution. Suppose that the set of moments chosen is called ξ and the transition of these moments

---

[32] I experiment with log-linearly interpolating along the x and n dimensions, but the results are similar in the steady state.

[33] See Bils et al. (2011), Elsby and Michaels (2013), and Fujita and Nakajima (2009) for examples of using this method in similar contexts.

is governed by γ. Therefore, Ξ is replaced by ξ in the dynamic programming problem to make the problem computable.

$$\Pi(n_{-1}, \ell_{-1}, x, p, \xi) = \max_n \left\{ pxF(n) - wn - \tau(\ell)wn - \frac{c}{q}\mathbf{1}^+ \Delta n \right.$$
$$\left. + \beta \int \int \Pi(n, \ell, x', p', \gamma(\xi)) dG(x'|x) dP(p'|p) \right\}. \quad (35)$$

The task is to solve for the transition equation: $\xi' = \gamma(p, \xi)$. I assume the moments are the mean of the employment distribution, $\bar{N}$, and the mean of the layoff distribution, $\bar{L}$ and conjecture log-linear transition equations

$$\ln \bar{L}' = \gamma_{\ell 0} + \gamma_{\ell 1} \ln \bar{L} + \gamma_{\ell 2} \ln \bar{N} + \gamma_{\ell 3} \ln p$$
$$\ln \bar{N}' = \gamma_{N 0} + \gamma_{N 1} \ln \bar{L} + \gamma_{N 2} \ln \bar{N} + \gamma_{N 3} \ln p.$$

Note that the firm takes these forecasts for the aggregate state and estimates labor market tightness in order to calculate expected future vacancy posting costs. That is the last equation

$$\ln \theta' = \gamma_{\theta 0} + \gamma_{\theta 1} \ln \bar{L}' + \gamma_{\theta 2} \ln \bar{N}' + \gamma_{\theta 3} \ln p'.$$

The solution algorithm is to find the parameters, γ, that accurately forecast aggregate variables. I discretize p via the method of Tauchen (1986) and solve the value function on the state space: $\{n, \ell, x, p, \bar{N}, \bar{L}, \theta, \xi\}$. I simulate the model for 10,000 firms and 2,000 periods and estimate the coefficients via OLS on the simulated data.

In practice, the means of the distribution provide adequate information for the firm to forecast the distribution of firms across states as measured by the sufficiently high R^2's in the regressions for the forecast coefficients. Higher R^2's would be obtained through either larger simulation sizes or with additional terms in the forecasting equations.

In the present model, market clearing every period is defined through an equilibrium labor market tightness that coincides with the flows of workers into and out of unemployment. In the standard Krusell and Smith (1998) model, market clearing is insured by the set up of the model—the labor market clears in every period as unemployment is exogenously determined. In the present model, however, the equilibrium for the labor market must be determined in every stage of the simulation.

In principle, firms know the aggregate state of the economy $\{p, \bar{N}, \bar{L}\}$ and can therefore predict equilibrium θ. However, forecast errors can lead to a situation in which the true market clearing level of θ is different from the forecasted level. Therefore, firms forecast θ from the equation using the guess for γ_θ, but I solve the value function on a grid of θ's. Then, in every time period of the simulation, I iteratively solve for the market clearing θ, $\bar{N}$, and $\bar{L}$. Further details as well as the

R^2's from the solution of the baseline model are given in Appendix B.

5.5 Calibration

A model period is calibrated to be one month in length. There are several parameters that are set externally before determining other parameters. I set $\beta = .996$ corresponding to an annual interest rate of 5%. The curvature of the production function, α, is set at .59. Average labor productivity is normalized to one in steady state. The elasticity of the matching function, ϕ, is set to .6 following Petrongolo and Pissarides (2001) and the bargaining parameter, η is set to .4, which is in the range used in the literature. Using a value of $\eta < \phi$ implies an unemployment rate inefficiently below the Hosios condition unemployment rate, which implies the effects of on unemployment in the tax experiments belows are not driven by an inefficiently high unemployment rate.

I now turn to the calibration of the other parameters of the model. The calibration strategy of the standard parameters borrows from Elsby and Michaels (2013). Table 9 contains a full list of the calibrated parameters, their meaning, and the moment they target. Fourteen parameters remain to be calibrated: $\mathbb{L}$, the size of the labor force; σ^x and ρ_x, the parameters of the idiosyncratic shock process; σ^p, ρ_p, the parameters of the aggregate shock process; b, the flow value of unemployment; c, the flow cost of vacancy posting; μ, the level of matching efficiency; δ, the depreciation of layoffs; $\underline{\tau}$, $\bar{\tau}$, the minimum and maximum tax rates; $\underline{\ell}$ $\bar{\ell}$, the tax schedule thresholds; MTC, the marginal tax cost. I now discuss each of these parameters in turn.

The job finding rate for the United States is targeted at 45% per month on average (Shimer (2005)). In addition, I follow Pissarides (2007) and target labor market tightness in steady state at .72. These two targets pin down matching efficiency, μ, according to the following relationship

$$f = \mu \theta^{1-\phi} \Rightarrow \mu = \frac{.45}{.72^{1-.6}} = .5132.$$

Firms take aggregate labor market tightness, θ, as given when determining optimal labor demand. In order to set steady state tightness at .72, I fix the labor force so that aggregate hiring implies a labor market tightness of .72. In other words, I set $\mathbb{L}$ according to the following steady state relationship

$$H = (\mathbb{L} - \bar{N})f \Rightarrow \mathbb{L} = \frac{H}{f} + \bar{N} \Rightarrow \mathbb{L} = \frac{H}{m\theta^{1-\phi}} + \bar{N}.$$

The shock process for idiosyncratic productivity consists of two parameters: the standard deviation of innovations to $\ln(x)$, σ^x, and the persistence of $\ln(x)$, ρ^x. In order to pin these parameters down, I target two moments from the QCEW data. First, the persistence of shocks, conditional on other parameters, will determine the extent of employment changes in equilibrium. If shocks are long-lived, firms will adjust less frequently. I follow Elsby and Michaels (2013) and target the fraction of employment adjustments that are less than 5% at a quarterly frequency. In the QCEW, this moment is 54.5% at a quarterly frequency.

The standard deviation of innovations controls the degree of job creation and job destruction in the model. The intuition for this is that the higher the standard deviation of shocks, the larger is the fraction of workers that are shed and hired in steady state. In the QCEW, the job reallocation rate, the sum of job creation and job destruction, is 12.5% per quarter. Therefore, I target the model job reallocation rate to pin down σ^x.

For a given set of parameters, further, the reservation productivity for shedding workers is decreasing in the value of leisure, b, due to the wage bargain. Therefore, a higher b will lead to a higher separation rate. I target a monthly separation rate of 3.12%. Along with a finding rate of 45%, this implies a steady state unemployment rate of 6.48%.

The flow cost of posting a vacancy imposes a hiring cost on the firm to the extent that each vacancy takes time to be filled. I target an estimate of hiring costs in Silva and Toledo (2005). They find that hiring costs are roughly 14% of average quarterly wages. Hiring costs in the model are given by $\frac{c}{q(\theta)}$, so I choose c to make this hiring cost 14% of quarterly wages.

I target the persistence of average labor productivity of $\rho^p = .983$ to coincide with a persistence of output per hour of about .95 quarterly. In addition, I choose the standard deviation of aggregate productivity shocks of $\sigma^p = .005$ to generate a standard deviation of average labor productivity at roughly 2%.

UI finance calibration and calculation of MTC

I now turn to calibration of the UI experience rating tax system. Recall that the marginal tax cost is the present discounted value of a dollar in benefits paid back in taxes. The marginal tax cost is calculated in the data for a firm always on the sloped portion of the schedule. I calculate the analogous measure in the model. Consider exogenously increasing a firm's layoff stock by one. This laid off worker receives unemployment benefits, b, for each period he is unemployed. In expectation, therefore, he receives $\frac{b}{1-\beta(1-f)}$ in present discounted value of unemployment benefits. On the other hand, the firm pays increased taxes of $\tau_c w n$ for this worker with a depreciation rate of $(1-\delta)$ each period. Therefore, the proportion of increased taxes paid back by the firm is the analogue to the empirical marginal tax cost. It is given by

$$MTC = \zeta \frac{\tau_c \bar{w} n}{b},$$

where $\zeta = \frac{1-\beta(1-f)}{1-\beta(1-\delta)}$.[34] In this formula, the average wage bill, $\bar{w}n$ is from the simulation for firms on the sloped schedule. From this equation, it is clear that the marginal tax cost is proportional to slope of the tax schedule, as it is in the data.

---

[34]χ, which was the empirical parameter for the fraction of benefits charged to firms is equal to 1 in the model.

In addition, δ helps determine the steady state distribution of firms across UI tax rates. In turn, $\underline{\ell}$ and $\bar{\ell}$ determines the slope of the tax schedule, given minimum and maximum tax rates. I set the minimum and maximum statutory rates as the average minimum and maximum rates across states in 2010 (weighted by employment). This implies a value of $\underline{\tau} = .042\%$ and $\bar{\tau} = 8.44\%$. It is important to discuss these tax rates in more detail. As discussed above, firms pay these payroll taxes only on a capped portion of payroll, ranging between $7,000 and $37,000. I abstract from the capped payroll in the model for simplicity. Using a tax rate proportional to total payroll is another potential calibration strategy. Since I target a marginal tax cost to the data, the level of the tax rates should not affect the quantitative results given an appropriately re-calibrated marginal tax cost.

All things equal, the parameter δ helps to pin down the distribution of firms across tax rates. Across states in 2010, an average of 17.7% and 6.7% of firms paid the minimum and maximum tax rates, respectively (again using the employment-weighted average). I choose δ to mimic this distribution of tax rates.

Model outcomes

The target moments along with their calibrated outcomes are listed in Table 10. Overall, the model moments are relatively close to their targets. In the worst case, I undershoot the fraction of employment changes that are small as well as the average quarterly job flow rate. In particular, the fraction of adjustments less than 5% is only 45% in the model as opposed to 54% in the data. In addition, the equilibrium job reallocation rate is 7.05% which is substantially lower than 12.5% in the QCEW data. The reason for the low model moments for each is that increasing the standard deviation of the idiosyncratic productivity reduces the fraction of small adjustments. In order to more accurately capture the cross-sectional distribution of employment growth, a richer model of persistent differences across firms is likely necessary.[35]

In addition, the separation rate in steady state is slightly higher than the targeted rate at 3.5% vs. 3.1%. This implies a steady state unemployment rate of 7.27% vs. a target of 6.5%. Hiring costs as a fraction of quarterly wages is near its target at 14.7%. The simulated process for average labor productivity is slightly less persistent (.94) and slightly less volatile (.0172) than in the data.[36] The distribution of firms across taxes is very close to the data, as shown in Figure 7. Roughly 17.43% (compared to 17.7% in the data) of firms are subject to the minimum rate while 6.76% (compared to 6.6%) are subject to the maximum rate.

---

[35] Elsby and Michaels (2013), for instance, consider the Pareto distribution for idiosyncratic shocks and include persistent firm fixed effects to better match the cross-section of firms.

[36] Due to the computational intensity of solving the approximate equilibrium, converging on the precise process for average labor productivity in simulated data is impractical.

6 Experience Rating Experiments

6.1 Steady State Comparative Statics

In this section, I show comparative statics from changes to the tax schedule that each raise the marginal tax cost. In particular, I study the equilibrium impact of a tax change on the rate of job creation and destruction, unemployment, and firm profits. Importantly, the model is not calibrated to match the empirical effect of experience rating on job flows; in part, these experiments will test the empirical results, as well as shed light on broader labor market effects.

The results provide new estimates of the effect of different channels to increase experience rating which could not be addressed in the previous literature that only modeled linear firing costs. The reason for this is two-fold. First, modeling the institution as a linear firing cost ignores the fundamental fact that firms must pay a payroll tax. Any level increase in payroll taxes reduces labor demand and therefore potentially offset the benefits of a higher layoff cost. Second, the simple linear firing cost ignores important firm heterogeneity across the tax schedule. This is important to accurately measure the revenue effects of tax changes. Suppose that all firms were at the minimum rate. Then increasing the maximum tax rate would have very little, if any, effect on tax revenues while still possibly changing layoff incentives.

The marginal tax cost in the model is calculated as in the data: it is the fraction of benefits paid back in taxes. Recall that in the model and the data, the marginal tax cost is proportional to the slope of the tax schedule. In the model, that implies the following relationship to the parameters of the tax schedule

$$MTC \propto \tau_c \equiv \underbrace{\left(\frac{\bar{\tau} - \underline{\tau}}{\bar{\ell} - \underline{\ell}}\right)}_{\text{slope}}.$$

Different possible changes to the slope are shown in Figure 8—they include an increase in the lower threshold, $\underline{\ell}$; a decrease in the minimum tax rate, $\underline{\tau}$; a decrease in the upper threshold, $\bar{\ell}$; or an increase in the maximum tax rate, $\bar{\tau}$. The experiments are run as follows. I adjust each parameter so as to increase the marginal tax cost by 5%. I then find the new equilibrium steady state (i.e., the equilibrium tightness) with the higher marginal tax cost. The results are shown in Table 11.

For each of the changes to the slope of the tax schedule, job creation and job destruction fall, with magnitudes quantitatively similar to the empirical results. Job creation and job destruction rates fall between 1.1% to 1.9% due to a 5% increase in MTC in the model. To compare, Table 2 shows that a 5% increase in MTC decreases job creation by 1.5% and job destruction about 2% in the baseline specification.[37] The effect on the unemployment rate is also negative in each of these

---

[37]These calculations are done by multiplying the coefficient on JD (-2.4) by .05 and dividing by 6.48, for instance.

specifications, but the magnitude depends on the relative effect on the change in tax revenues.[38]

The reason that unemployment falls between -0.02 ppt and -.31 ppt is due to the associated change in the tax burden on firms. For experiments in which the average tax burden on firms rises, overall labor demand falls, mitigating the effect of lower job destruction. Overall, unemployment still falls in each experiment regardless of the change in tax receipts. Larger decreases in unemployment are consistent, however, with reducing taxes. Moving the upper threshold to the left or increasing the maximum tax rate *increases* the tax rate on many firms. For instance, moving the lower threshold to the right or the minimum tax down *reduces* tax revenue by 8.6% in each case. On the other hand, decreasing the upper threshold or raising the maximum rate actually increases revenue by 2.3%.

Increasing taxes while reducing unemployment might appear at first to constitute a Pareto improvement. In column 6 of Table 11, however, I find that the average enterprise value of firms falls in experiments in which taxes are increased.[39] Row four is the experiment that decreases unemployment the most while still raising tax revenue. In this case, profits fall by about .4%. In the case that both taxes fall and unemployment falls by the most (three tenths of a percent, row 3), profits increase by about .07%. Therefore, there is an offsetting effect of lower firm profits when tax revenues are increased.[40]

Implications for UI Financing

Net UI reserves were in their worst financial position at the end of 2011, registering -0.5% as a fraction of payroll. This was the third consecutive year of negative reserves and the longest streak of negative reserves since the program's inception. Vroman (2012) notes that UI reserves as a fraction of payrolls were particularly hard hit during the Great Recession due to the lowest run-up of reserves in the expansion prior to the 2007 recession.[41]

The results of the previous section show that different changes to the UI tax schedule imply differing effects on tax revenues and the labor market. These experiments naturally have important policy implications for reforming UI trust fund financing, a topic that is currently on the legislative

---

[38]The job finding rate increases by small percentages in the second and fourth columns (.8% and 1.2% respectively, not shown). In the first and third row, the job finding rate increases by 3.6% and 5.3%.

[39]I calculate this comparative static by taking the average across the firm's value function in equation 17. The results are quantitatively similar by comparing flow profits.

[40]Given that the unemployment rate falls in both experiments in which tax revenue is increased, it is possible to alter experience rating in a revenue neutral fashion and still decrease unemployment. This could be done, for example, in the following way. Start from the experiment of raising the maximum tax rate in the fourth row of Table 11. In that experiment, $\bar{\tau}$ increased by .4 percentage points to raise the marginal tax cost by 5%, which raised tax revenues by 2.3% in the new steady state. To achieve revenue neutrality, one could iteratively lower the minimum tax rate until revenues return to steady state. Even in this experience, unemployment will fall.

[41]Vroman (2012) suggests that all states index the taxable payroll cap to wage growth at the state level, as is currently done in sixteen states. While indexation is a very important channel for UI financing reform, this paper has abstracted from the taxable cap on wages and has focused on the shape of the tax schedule and the experience rating formula in determining UI financing.

agenda at both the national and state levels. Changes to the tax schedule are being considered by many states in order to ensure more adequate UI financing in the future. Some states, such as New York and New Jersey have considered levying flat rate fees on all employers or raising both the minimum and maximum tax rates. States have not considered increasing the degree of experience rating on high-rated employers, however. Alan Krueger (2008) has proposed increasing the degree of experience rating, saying: "Unfortunately, the degree of experience rating has severely lapsed. Improved experience rating would discourage employers from laying off workers, and help to internalize the externalities layoffs impose on society."

In this section, I study two different methods for shoring-up UI financing to close half of the net reserve deficit (an increase of revenue equivalent to .25% of payroll). This amounts to a one-time increase of 9.1% of revenue in the baseline, calibrated model. I will compare the labor market effects of a level shift to the tax schedule versus a revenue-equivalent increase in the slope of the tax schedule by shifting $\bar{\ell}$ to the left. The level shift of the tax schedule is of the type being considered in many states, either implemented as an increase in all tax rates or as flat levies on all firms.

In order to raise revenue by 9.1% in a level-shift of the tax schedule, the intercept of the schedule needs to be increased by 0.2 percentage points, making the minimum tax rate 0.617% and the maximum rate 8.64%. In the second experiment, I reduce the upper threshold, $\bar{\ell}$ by 12.4%. Table 12 shows the new labor market outcomes under these two experiments.

In the first row, under the experiment in which the tax schedule is raised uniformly, unemployment increases by about a tenth of a percentage point in order to raise revenue 9.1%. Under the experiment in which the slope is increased, the marginal tax cost increases by 19%. In this experiment, states would raise revenue by 9.1% again while actually improving labor market conditions and reducing unemployment by 0.13 percentage points.

While the previous experiments were two examples of equal revenue-enhancing policy changes, they are not "reserve equivalent". The first experiment increases unemployment, thereby increasing payments of unemployment benefits by 1.5%. The net change in reserves is therefore 7.6% while in the second experiment, the net change in reserves is 10.9%.[42]

6.2 Aggregate Dynamics

The previous section showed the steady state effects of a change in experience rating. In this section, I analyze the dynamics of the labor market in response to aggregate shocks. Due to experience-rated taxes, firms are reluctant to lay off workers and face higher tax rates. The layoff cost dampens the response of the labor market to aggregate shocks. Due to accumulated layoffs and the resulting higher tax burden, the model also exhibits non-linearities and asymmetries in the unemployment

---

[42]Unemployment benefits simply equal $u \times b$ so the percentage increase (decrease) in benefits is just the percentage increase (decrease) in the unemployment rate given in the last column. Therefore, the change in reserves is just the change in revenues (column 5) minus column 8.

response to aggregate shocks.

I now turn to understanding the quantitative effect of experience rating on the labor market after an aggregate productivity shock. I construct impulse responses to a decline in aggregate productivity under different tax schedules. For each tax experiment, I re-solve the approximate aggregate equilibrium forecast equations. I then simulate the path of endogenous variables following a temporary 1% decline in aggregate productivity.

In Figure 9, I plot the impulse responses of productivity, unemployment, the separation rate, and the finding rate for two different marginal tax costs, 51% and 56.7% (5% above and below the baseline of 54%). I choose to vary the upper threshold of the tax schedule, $\bar{\ell}$ in order to achieve the change in the marginal tax cost. Note here that I am being conservative in this choice as the effect of varying this parameter had the smallest effect on steady state unemployment. Examining the dashed lines first, in response to a 1% aggregate shock, the unemployment increases on impact and peaks after two quarters, increasing to about 11% above its steady state.[43]

The increase in unemployment is driven by a spike in separations on impact. This is shown in the bottom left panel of Figure 9. Here we see that the separation rate increases by just over 10% on impact but declines quickly, as is standard in endogenous separation models. In addition, the job finding rate falls as workers exit to unemployment and vacancy posting falls. The job finding rate falls by just over 6% and also takes two quarters to reach its nadir. In contrast to similar models without experience rating, the job finding rate (and labor market tightness) does not peak on impact. This is seen in the fact that the job finding rate reaches its trough in the second quarter after the shock. The inclusion of experience rating appears to add modest propagation of shocks since it takes time for firms to recover from the higher tax rates.

Comparing the impulse responses under the two tax schedules shows that a higher marginal tax cost reduces the amplitude of recessions. The higher marginal tax cost impulse responses are depicted by the solid lines. Instead of unemployment increasing by 11%, unemployment increases by 6.8% less, a difference of about .045 percentage points. In addition, the separation rate increases by 7.8% more and the job finding rate falls by 3.3% more under lower experience rating. The results in this section show that experience rating in fact stabilizes employment by reducing separations and mitigating the effect of recessions on unemployment.

Since the layoff cost in UI financing is on the *stock* of accumulated layoffs, it is possible that this system induces non-linearities in the response of the labor market to larger shocks. In order to examine this further, I show the impulse response of unemployment to a two and three percent negative shock to productivity. I plot the impulse responses keeping the marginal tax cost constant at 56.7% from the previous experiment (solid blue lines). In order to make the one, two, and three percent shock responses comparable, I halve and third the responses to the two and three percent

---

[43]It is worth noting that the impulse response of unemployment is similar in magnitude to those shown in similar models such Fujita and Nakajima (2009).

shocks given by the red-dashed line and the black line with circles shown in Figure 10. From this figure, we can see that there is more non-linearity in the impulse responses than is typically found in similar models, such as Elsby and Michaels (2013) and Fujita and Nakajima (2009). Since firms have accumulated a larger stock of layoffs, unemployment does not decline as quickly from the larger shock; the largest difference between these two responses is, in fact, in the 6th quarter after the shock. Because firms are still coping with higher taxes from the recession-induced shock to layoffs, the path of recovery of unemployment is relatively slower. Comparing the two and three percent shocks, the model also generates additional propagation in response to larger shocks—the unemployment rate only peaks after the third quarter in response to the three percent shock whereas the peak was at two quarters in response to the smaller shocks. These results provide an explanation, rooted in tax policy, for some part of the persistence of unemployment and vacancies that traditional models cannot easily capture.

In addition to non-linearities, experience rating introduces important asymmetries between positive and negative shocks. First, comparing the solid lines in Figures 9 and 11, it is clear that the impulse response to the negative shock induces a much larger recession than the positive shock causes a boom. This is due mostly to the asymmetric affect on the separation rate which rises by 10% from a negative shock but only falls by 4.5% after a positive shock. There is also asymmetry in the effect of experience rating. In Figure 9, the finding rates react relatively similarly regardless of the marginal tax cost. In response to the boom, higher experience rating has a substantial effect on the finding rate behavior. The higher marginal tax cost causes the finding rate to rise by almost 10% less (.3 percentage points) and stays about 15% lower for twelve quarters relative to the lower marginal tax cost economy. The strong effect on the finding rate in the higher marginal tax cost example is due to the fact that firms anticipate that the boom times are temporary. If they hire a lot of workers but subsequently must lay them off as the shock dissipates, they will owe a substantial fraction in increased UI taxes. Therefore, higher experience rating dampens the effects of a positive shock when firms expect to lay off workers as the boom fades.

Moreover, the experience rating system does not induce the same type of nonlinear response of unemployment to positive shocks. In Figure 12, I plot the impulse response of unemployment to positive one, two, and three percent shocks, and scale the impulse responses accordingly (as in Figure 10). Here, we do not see the same type of proportionally larger responses to larger shocks. While the two- and three- percent impulse responses are somewhat larger than the one percent, the two and three percent lines lie one top of each other. This is due to the fact that in response to booms, layoffs fall and there is no added effect of higher taxes due to the large stock of layoffs accumulated over the business cycle.

6.3 Endogenous Depreciation of Layoffs

Up until this point, the depreciation rate of layoffs has been assumed to be a constant. Recall that layoffs depreciate for two reasons: (1) due to statutory limits on the duration of time that benefits are counted on a firm's books and (2) because laid off workers find other jobs. This suggests, therefore, that the rate of deprecation of layoffs should be a function of the exit rate from unemployment, $\delta \equiv \delta(f(\theta))$. Data on this variation, however, is unavailable. I make the assumption that the depreciation rate differs from its baseline steady state level in proportion with the deviation of the job finding rate from the calibrated steady state value of .45. The equation for the log depreciation rate is therefore

$$\ln(\delta_t) = \ln(\bar{\delta}) + \kappa_\delta \left[\ln(f_t) - \ln(\bar{f}) \right], \qquad (36)$$

where $\kappa_\delta \in [0, 1]$ and $\bar{x}$ is the steady state value of a variable from the baseline calibration.

In this section, I conduct the same tax experiments allowing for varying deprecation of layoffs. Note that this captures the important features of a varying depreciation rate: when the finding rate is higher than normal, laid off workers find jobs at a quicker rate and therefore remain on the firm's book for less time, implying a higher depreciation rate. For the purposes of this section, I show results setting $\kappa_\delta = 25\%$ to demonstrate that the qualitative results of the previous section are bolstered when allowing endogenous depreciation.[44]

The depreciation rate varies both in the steady state experiments of Table 11 as well as over the course of the business cycle. In the steady state experiments, allowing the deprecation rate to vary with the finding rate amplifies the effect of each of the experiments on the unemployment rate. This is for the simple reason that the finding rate rises and therefore the depreciation rate increases. This in turn shifts the distribution of layoffs in equilibrium to lower tax rates and reduces total tax revenues collected.

Table 13 shows the results from each of the four experiments with endogenous depreciation. In each of the four experiments, the drop in the unemployment rate is amplified due to the fall in the depreciation rate as the distribution of layoffs shifts to lower tax rates in the new steady state. Job flows fall between three-tenths of a point and 1.1 points more with varying depreciation. Unemployment now falls between 0.2 points up to almost 0.6 points from 0.13 and 0.33 with a fixed depreciation rate, respectively.

The reason for these larger effects is that the reduction in revenues can be quite large. In the first and third rows, the drop of 8.6% in revenues from Table 11 is amplified to about an 18% drop with varying depreciation. In the second row, the change in revenue remains almost the same, but

---

[44]One practical reason that I did not choose $\kappa_\delta = 1$ is that the grid used in numerical simulations with fixed depreciation are not well suited when δ can vary widely. In addition, some states restrict the degree to which a firm's tax burden can rise or fall over the business cycle, potentially mitigating the effect of the finding rate on the firm's taxes.

the increase in the depreciation rate is small (1.5%). Figure 13 plots the cross-sectional distribution of taxes under the low $\underline{\tau}$ experiment, fixing δ and allowing δ to vary with the finding rate. Here, we can see a substantial increase in the mass at the lower tax rate. This shift of mass to the lower tax rate accounts for the large drop in revenues in rows 1 and 3 of Table 11. From a policy perspective, the loss in revenue from the endogenous depreciation of layoffs can be counteracted by extending the amount of time that benefits are charged to the firm. In essence, the experiments in Table 11 assumed that the state re-adjusts the depreciation rate back to 2.6%.

As the finding rate varies over the business cycle, the rate at which previous layoffs find new jobs varies substantially. In this case, during a recession when the finding rate falls, a firm's stock of layoffs should be expected to remain higher for longer. Endogenous depreciation, therefore, can reduce the firm's incentive to lay off works in response to a negative shock. In order to examine this effect of the experience rating system, I solve a version of the model in which the depreciation rate varies according to equation 36. Since the endogenous depreciation rate is determined by the finding rate, and in turn, labor market tightness, I do not need to add a forecast equation to the Krusell & Smith algorithm. Forecasting tightness is sufficient for the firm to forecast deviations in depreciation.[45] I then plot impulse responses to a 1% negative aggregate productivity shock.

In Figure 14, I compare three different impulse responses: (1) under high experience rating and fixed depreciation (crossed, green line), (2) under high experience rating and varying depreciation (solid, blue line), and (3) under low experience rating and varying depreciation (dashed, red line). The crossed line is identical to the solid line in Figure 9. The bottom left panel plots the response of the depreciation rate—the crossed line remains as the steady state while the depreciation rate falls with the finding rate in the other two economies.

Figure 14 shows that varying depreciation also amplifies the effect of experience rating over the business cycle. First, consider the difference in the blue line with and MTC of 56.7% and varying depreciation compared to the crossed line with the $MTC = 56.7\%$ and fixed depreciation. We can see that the unemployment rate spikes by less under varying depreciation since the separation rate (middle left panel) spikes by less.

In addition, the unemployment impulse response exhibits additional propagation in two ways. First, it takes unemployment in the economy with varying depreciation three quarters as opposed to two to peak from the shock. Then the shock dissipates more slowly—the crossed line catches up to the solid line at around 11 quarters. The reason for this is the faster depreciation of layoffs and thus lower taxes after the shock fades away. In the middle right panel, we can see that the layoff stock without varying depreciation is substantially lower than with varying depreciation, *even though* there was a larger bout of job destruction.

---

[45]The goodness of fit of the Krusell & Smith regressions with varying depreciation is quantitatively similar to those in the baseline solution.

7 Related Literature

Brechling (1975) and Feldstein (1976) were two of the earliest examinations of the theoretical implications of experience rating. Feldstein (1976) found that an imperfect experience rating system in which firms did not pay the full cost of benefits (i.e., the MTC is less than 100%) accounted for a large portion of temporary layoffs and the resulting unemployment from an economic downturn. In a series of seminal papers, Topel (1983, 1984) first studied the empirical effects of imperfect experience rating. Exploiting state variation in the marginal tax cost, Topel found that firms only pay around 75% of benefits charged. Using Current Population Survey (CPS) data along with state UI tax schedules, he shows that layoffs could be reduced by 20% with perfect experience rating. Card and Levine (1994) also study the effect of higher marginal tax costs on layoff rates. They find that full experience rating would reduce layoffs at a higher rate in recessionary periods.

Anderson (1993) and Anderson and Meyer (2000) study the effect of experience rating in the context of a linear layoff cost model. Anderson (1993) is one of the only papers to use micro-level data to study the effect of experience rating. Anderson finds that the presence of the linear adjustment cost due to experience rating decreases the response of employment changes to seasonal variation—the labor market is less volatile because of the experience rating. In addition, she finds that the level of employment is slightly higher on average. In fact, moving to perfect experience rating would increase employment by 4.3% over the seasonal cycle.

The general equilibrium effect of layoff costs on employment depend crucially on the structure of the labor market, as shown by Ljungqvist (2002). Albrecht and Vroman (1999) further show in an efficiency wage model, experience rating reduces unemployment relative to a model with privately financed unemployment insurance. On the other hand, Hopenhayn and Rogerson (1993) find that linear layoff costs reduce employment, although their model abstracts from search frictions and instead considers employment determined by lotteries. In the context of search models, Millard and Mortensen (1996) show that layoff costs unambiguously reduce both job creation and job destruction but the overall effect on employment is ambiguous depending on which effect dominates. Lower unemployment in search and matching models with endogenous job destruction is driven by reduced job reallocation externalities at the cost of a potentially less efficient allocation of labor.

This paper finds that higher layoff costs reduces unemployment. In a labor market without search frictions, such as in Hopenhayn and Rogerson (1993), there is no externality caused by layoffs. Lower employment is generated by workers substituting towards leisure since the private gain from employment is reduced from lower wages. In search models, externalities arise since each layoff clogs the market for searchers through lower finding rates. Therefore, it can be the case that in equilibrium, layoff costs reduce the rate of reallocation in the labor market and therefore reduces the unemployment rate.

Several additional papers explore experience rating in the context of search models. First, l'Haridon and Malherbet (2009) study UI finance in a standard job search model. The firing cost from experience rating, unlike in this paper, is exogenously determined. They also find that higher experience rating reduces the unemployment rate. In more recent theoretical work, Albertini (2011) studies the reserve ratio experience rating system in a search model. Albertini (2011) is the only other paper to tie the firm's tax rate to its experience. Similarly, he finds that higher experience rating reduces the amplitude of recessions. This model, however, does not model heterogeneity in firms and instead uses a representative agent framework. The model, therefore, is less suited to study the tax incidence from changes in experience rating as a richer model with heterogeneity allows.

8 Conclusion

The United States finances unemployment insurance with an experience-rated tax system in which firms are penalized for layoffs with higher tax rates. In this paper, I study the labor market effects of experience rating of UI taxes, empirically and theoretically. I show that a model of labor demand under experience-rated taxes predicts that both the rates of job creation and job destruction fall with higher experience rating. The intuition for this is that firms face a positive marginal cost of a layoff and therefore have an incentive to minimize layoffs. Because of the possibility of laying off a newly-hired worker, experience rating can also act as a hiring deterrent.

This paper is the first to examine the relationship between experience rating and job flows. I confirm the model prediction using firm-level data from the Quarterly Census of Employment and Wages. I find robust evidence that higher experience rating reduces job destruction and job creation, leading to a decrease in total job reallocation in the labor market. In the baseline specification, I find that going from average marginal tax cost to 100% marginal tax cost would reduce job destruction by 17%, job creation by 13.7%, and job reallocation by about 10%.

I then embed experience rating into a DSGE model with search unemployment. Using this model, I conduct steady state tax experiments. I find that higher experience rating reduces job flows as well as reduces unemployment. Quantitatively, the model predicts that job flows fall by roughly the same amount as is predicted by the empirical results. The relative effect on unemployment depends on the type of tax change. Those that reduce tax revenues have a larger effect on unemployment while those that raise revenues reduce unemployment by far less. In experiments that raise revenue, I also find that there is a small decrease in firm profits.

Finally, I solve the model with aggregate uncertainty using the method of Krusell and Smith (1998). I find that the labor market response to an aggregate shock is dampened by higher experience rating as firms do not shed as many workers in response to the shock. With a 10% higher marganal tax cost, unemployment increases by 0.045 percentage points (7%) less upon impact of the shock. Since the layoff cost is a function of the accumulated stock of layoffs, experience rating introduces nonlinear effects from larger shocks. It takes unemployment longer to recover from larger shocks since firms must shed the relatively larger overhang of accumulated layoffs. I also find that higher experience rating has a substantial and asymmetric effect on firms' hiring behavior from a positive shock relative to a negative shock. Since firms expect the boom to be temporary, any current hires will have to be laid off as the economy returns to steady state. Therefore, the job finding rate spikes substantially less from a positive shock relative to a negative one. Lastly, I show that allowing the depreciation rate of layoffs to vary with the finding rate makes the bite of experience rating over the business more stringent and thus further dampens business cycles.

For the present study, the welfare analysis of these changes is not addressed. There are at least two caveats to inferring welfare gains from the results in this paper. Since the model above abstracts from on-the-job search and heterogeneity in workers, there may be reasons that workers benefit from reallocation, such as finding better job matches. If this is the case, then it is not clear reducing job flows is welfare enhancing.

Moreover, I have assumed that the government does not impose distortionary taxes to fill any holes in UI financing. In practice, states and the federal government typically use general revenue funds to fill gaps in UI funding. If changing experience rating imposes an additional burden of distortionary taxes, the effects on the labor market and welfare may be different. However, the paper suggest that states might alter tax schedules to help plug UI trust fund deficits without harming the economic recovery in the labor market.

References

ABEL, A. AND J. EBERLY (1996): "Optimal Investment with Costly Reversibility," *The Review of Economic Studies*, 63.

ABOWD, J., P. CORBEL, AND F. KRAMARZ (1999): "The Entry and Exit of Workers and the Growth of Employment: An Analysis of French Establishments," *Review of Economics and Statistics*, 81, 170–187.

ALBERTINI, J. (2011): "Unemployment insurance payroll tax, matching frictions and the labor market dynamics," University of Evry, Mimeo.

ALBRECHT, J. AND S. VROMAN (1999): "Unemployment compensation finance and efficiency wages," *Journal of Labor Economics*, 141–167.

ANDERSON, P. M. (1993): "Linear Adjustment Costs and Seasonal Labor Demand: Evidence from Retail Trade Firms." *The Quarterly Journal of Economics*, 108.

ANDERSON, P. M. AND B. D. MEYER (1993): "Unemployment Insurance in the United States: Layoff Incentives and Cross Subsidies," *Journal of Labor Economics*, 11.

——— (2000): "The effect of the unemployment insurance payroll tax on wages, employment, claims, and denials," *Journal of Public Economics*, 78.

BARLEVY, G. (2002): "The sullying effect of recessions," *Review of Economic Studies*, 69, 65–96.

BARNICHON, R. (2010): "The Lumpy Job Separation Rate," Federal Reserve Board Working Paper.

BILS, M., Y. CHANG, AND S.-B. KIM (2011): "Worker Heterogeneity and Endogenous Separations in a Matching Model of Unemployment Fluctuations," *American Economic Journal: Macroeconomics*, 3.

BRECHLING, F. (1975): "The Incentive Effect of U.S. Unemployment Insurance Tax." Public Research Institute.

BUREAU OF LABOR STATISTICS (2011): "Job Openings and Labor Turnover Survey," .

CABALLERO, R., E. ENGEL, AND J. HALTIWANGER (1997): "Aggregate Employment Dynamics: Building from Microeconomic Evidence," *American Economics Review*, 87.

CAHUC, P. AND F. MALBERHET (2002): "Unemployment Compensation Finance and Labor Market Rigidity," .

CARD, D. AND P. B. LEVINE (1994): "Unemployment Insurance Taxes and the Cyclical and Seasonal Properties of Unemployment," *Journal of Public Economics*, 52.

DAVIS, S. J., R. J. FABERMAN, AND J. HALTIWANGER (2006): "The Flow Approach to Labor Markets: New Data Sources and Micro-Macro Links," *The Journal of Economic Perspectives*, 20.

DAVIS, S. J., R. J. FABERMAN, J. HALTIWANGER, R. JARMIN, AND J. MIRANDA (2010): "Business Volatility, Job Destruction, and Unemployment," *American Economic Journal: Macroeconomics*, 2, 259–287.

DAVIS, S. J. AND J. HALTIWANGER (1992): "Gross Job Creation, Job Destruction, and Employment Reallocation," *The Quarterly Journal of Economics*, 107.

ELSBY, M. AND R. MICHAELS (2013): "Marginal jobs, heterogeneous firms, and unemployment flows," *American Economic Journal: Macroeconomics*, 5, 1–48.

FABERMAN, R. (2008): *Job flows, jobless recoveries, and the Great Moderation*, Federal Reserve Bank of Philadelphia.

FELDSTEIN, M. (1976): "Temporary layoffs in the theory of unemployment," *The Journal of Political Economy*, 937–957.

FUJITA, S. AND M. NAKAJIMA (2009): "Worker Flows and Job Flows: A Quantitative Investigation," .

GOLTZ, J. (2010): "Why the Payroll Tax Break Won't Creat Jobs," http://boss.blogs.nytimes.com/2010/01/27/why-the-payroll-tax-break-wont-create-jobs/.

HAMERMESH, D. AND G. PFANN (1996): "Adjustment costs in factor demand," *Journal of Economic Literature*, 34, 1264–1292.

HOPENHAYN, H. AND R. ROGERSON (1993): "Job turnover and policy evaluation: A general equilibrium analysis," *Journal of Political Economy*, 915–938.

KIYOTAKI, N. AND R. LAGOS (2007): "A Model of Job and Worker Flows," *Journal of Political Economy*, 115, 770–819.

KRUEGER, A. (2008): "Unemployment in a volatile economics: how to secure families and build opportunity," *Testimony before U.S. Senate Health, Education, Labor, and Pensions Committee*.

KRUSELL, P. AND A. SMITH, JR (1998): "Income and wealth heterogeneity in the macroeconomy," *Journal of Political Economy*, 106, 867–896.

L'HARIDON, O. AND F. MALHERBET (2009): "Employment Protection Reform in Search Economics," *European Economic Review*, 53, 255–273.

LJUNGQVIST, L. (2002): "How Do Lay-off Costs Affect Employment?" *The Economic Journal*, 829–853.

MCCONNELL, M. AND J. S. TRACY (2005): "Unemployment Insurance and the Diminished Importance of Temporary Layoffs Over the Business Cycle," .

MILLARD, S. AND D. MORTENSEN (1996): *Unemployment policy: How should governments respond to unemployment*, Cambridge University Press, chap. The unemployment and welfare effects of labour market policy: a comparison of the USA and the UK, 545–572.

MORTENSEN, D. T. AND C. PISSARIDES (2001): "Taxes Subsidies and Equilibrium Labor Market Outcomes," CEPR Discussion Paper No. 2989.

PAVOSEVICH, R. (2009): "Too Many Discounts in Unemployment Insurance Financing?" .

PETRONGOLO, B. AND C. PISSARIDES (2001): "Looking into the black box: A survey of the matching function," *Journal of Economic Literature*, 39, 390–431.

PETROSKY-NADEAU, N. AND L. ZHANG (2013): "Unemployment Crises," Carnegie Mellon University, mimeo.

PISSARIDES, C. (2000): *Equilibrium Unemployment Theory*, The MIT Press.

——— (2007): "The Unemployment Volatility Puzzle: Is Wage Stickiness the Answer?" *CEP Discussion Paper*.

SHIMER, R. (2001): "The Impact of Young Workers on the Aggregate Labor Market," *The Quarterly Journal of Economics*, 116, pp. 969–1007.

——— (2005): "The cyclical behavior of equilibrium unemployment and vacancies," *American economic review*, 25–49.

SILVA, J. AND M. TOLEDO (2005): "Labor Turnover Costs and the Cyclical Behavior of Vacancies and Unemployment," in *2005 Meeting Papers*, Society for Economic Dynamics.

STOLE, L. AND J. ZWIEBEL (1996): "Intra-firm bargaining under non-binding contracts," *The Review of Economic Studies*, 63, 375.

TAUCHEN, G. (1986): "Finite state Markov-chain approximations to univariate and vector autoregressions," *Economics letters*, 20, 177–181.

TOPEL, R. (1983): "On layoffs and unemployment insurance," *The American Economic Review*, 73, 541–559.

——— (1984): "Experience rating of unemployment insurance and the incidence of unemployment," *JL & Econ.*, 27, 61.

UNITED STATES DEPARTMENT OF LABOR (2010): "Comparison of State Unemployment Laws: Financing," *http://workforcesecurity.doleta.gov/unemploy/pdf/uilawcompar/2010/financing.pdf*.

——— (2012): "Unemployment Insurance Financial Data Handbook 394," *http://workforcesecurity.doleta.gov/unemploy/hb394.asp*.

VROMAN, W. (2009): "Unemployment Insurance: Current Situation and Potential Reforms," *Urban Institute*.

——— (2010): "The Role of Unemployment Insurance As an Automatic Stabilizer During a Recession," *IMPAQ International, LLC*.

——— (2011): "Unemployment Insurance: Problems and Prospects," *National Academy of Social Insurance*, Unemployment Insurance Brief.

——— (2012): "Unemployment Insurance Performance and Trust Fund Restoration," *Testimony before U.S. House of Representatives, Committee on Ways and Means, Subcommittee on Human Resources, April 25th 2012*.

WOODBURY, S. A. (2004): "Layoffs and Experience Rating of the Unemployment Insurance Payroll Tax: Panel Data Analysis of Employers in Three States," .

A Firm's Problem with Recall

In this section, I generalize the model to allow firms to rehire some of its laid off workers. I assume that laid off workers are recalled without the flow cost c. To maintain hiring from both the general pool of unemployed and the temporarily laid off, I assume that if a firm wanted to hire h workers, it may hire up to the proportion p^T from its stock of lay offs. I assume for simplicity that firms still post "vacancies" for each recall and meets those vacancies with rate q. Of those hired from outside its layoff pool, the firm posts a vacancy, v_r at a flow cost c. This allows me define the finding and queueing rates in the same manner as above.

The equations of motion and costs of hiring will depend on the size of the stock of layoffs relative to the desired level of hiring. I now describe these in more detail. Suppose that the firm considers hiring $\mathbb{1}^+\Delta n$ workers. If the fraction it will recall from ℓ is less than its stock available for recall, i.e. $p_T\mathbb{1}^+\Delta n < \ell_{-1}(1-\delta)$, then

$$(1-p^T)\mathbb{1}^+\Delta n = qv_r \to v_r = (1-p^T)\frac{\mathbb{1}^+\Delta n}{q}.$$

On the other hand, suppose that it wants to hire so many workers such that it depletes its stock of layoffs. Then, $p_T\mathbb{1}^+\Delta n \geq \ell_{-1}(1-\delta)$ and

$$\mathbb{1}^+\Delta n = \ell_{-1}(1-\delta) + qv_r \to v_r = \frac{\mathbb{1}^+\Delta n - \ell_{-1}(1-\delta)}{q}.$$

Notice that if $p_T = 0$, the first condition–$p_T\mathbb{1}^+\Delta n \leq \ell_{-1}(1-\delta)$–always holds and $v = \frac{\mathbb{1}^+\Delta n}{q}$, as in the standard model. We can now state the general equations of motion for the stock of layoffs for a firm

$$\ell = (1-\delta)\ell_{-1} - \underbrace{\mathbb{1}^-\Delta n}_{\text{layoffs}} - \underbrace{\min\{\mathbb{1}^+\Delta n p_T, (1-\delta)\ell_{-1}\}}_{\text{recalls}}, \quad \ell \geq 0.$$

Note that total vacancies are v_r plus the amount of recalls because of my assumption that each hire must be associated with a vacancy.

$$v = v_r + p^T\mathbb{1}^+\Delta n.$$

The addition of recalls reduces the cost of laying off a worker since you can rehire that worker without cost in the future. Consider the case where $p^T = 1$. In this case, firms can costlessly rehire from its stock of layoffs up to the point that it depletes its entire stock. Assuming a large enough stock, this reduces the firm's problem to the frictionless one. To see this, the equation of motion for ℓ becomes

$$\ell = (1-\delta)\ell_{-1} - \mathbb{1}^-\Delta n - \mathbb{1}^+\Delta n \to \ell = (1-\delta)\ell_{-1} - \Delta n.$$

In this case, there is no kink in the adjustment cost. At the point at which the firm recalls all of its workers, the marginal hire will cost c per vacancy and thus the firm behaves as in the standard linear hiring cost model. For $p^T < 1$, there remains a linear layoff cost, but its magnitude falls with p^T. The band of inaction shown in the policy functions in Figure 4 will correspondingly shrink with p^T.

I take the calibrated model of Section 6 and allow the firm to rehire up to 10% of its hires from its layoffs.[46] The steady state effects are as expected: the fraction of firms at both the low and high tax rates are higher. At the low tax rate, the mass increases from 17.43% to 18.27% and the low tax rate the perfect of firms changes from 6.76% to 7.75%. This is because firms are more likely to

---

[46]p^T is an unobservable parameter from standard sources of data on the labor market. Data from the CPS suggest that 17% is an upper bound on the fraction of hires that are from temporarily laid off workers. This fraction assumes that *all* temporarily laid off workers who are hired are hired by the firm that laid them off. Therefore, 10% is in the range of plausible values for p^T.

hold higher layoff stocks as the cost of that stock is lower due to the recall possibility. In addition, firms recall more of their layoffs and so more firms are at the low tax rate.

B Numerical Algorithm

This section describes in detail the steps to solve the steady state and aggregate uncertainty versions of the model. I start by describing the solution to the steady state model.

I solve the firm's problem by standard value function iteration on a discretized grid of its state variables. The firm's state variables are n, ℓ, x. I discretize the continuous choice variables n and ℓ into E_p and L_p points, respectively. The firms optimal decision for employment, conditional on its states, determines ℓ. I discretize ℓ independently of n, however, and piecewise linearly interpolate the value function at points off the ℓ grid. I restrict the firm to choose employment on the discretized grid. By virtue of choosing a fairly fine number of grid points (minimum of 75), this restriction does not substantially effect the firm's policy functions. Robustness checks using polynomial interpolation off the employment grid yield similar results.

Idiosyncratic shocks are assumed to be log-normally distributed. I therefore discretize the space of idiosyncratic shocks using Tauchen's method described in Carroll (2011).[47] Due to the highly nonlinear nature of the policy function from experience rating, I use at least 11 equiprobable points in the grid.

I start with a guess of Π^j. At each iteration I evaluate optimal choice conditional on not adjusting, hiring, or firing. I then take the max over those three possible choices as the updated guess for Π^{j+1}. If the maximum percentage deviation of Π^j and Π_{j+1} is less than a pre-specified tolerance, the value function has converged. I use the optimal choice at each grid point to define $n^* = \Phi(n, \ell, x')$, the policy function.

Armed with the policy function, I generate a simulated panel dataset of firms over T periods. I simulate the continuous log-AR(1) shock process and linearly interpolate the policy function to points off each grid. I ensure that during the simulation (after the system has settled into steady state) that each state variable remains on the grid so that no extrapolation procedure is needed. Extrapolating is subject to large approximation error as well as computational intensity. I restrict the points for x to remain on the grid. Due to the equiprobable choice of the grid, this happens with probability $\frac{1}{N_x+1}$. Experimentation with polynomial interpolation and linear interpolation in the logs (as opposed to levels) did not change the results substantially.

Calibration of the model is performed using a coarse grid search across the relevant state space and then a numerical minimization of the sum of squared residuals from the target moments. For this, I use the package *fminsearchbnd* which implements a simplex search method optimization routine. This method is often preferable to a gradient based method as it is more robust to

---

[47]I thank Ryan Michaels for the Matlab code to produce this discretization.

discontinuities in the objective function.

Finally, I conduct the steady state tax schedule experiments as follows. A new steady state of the model consists of finding a fixed point in θ–firms take the conjectured θ as given and this must be consistent with labor market tightness of the simulated panel of firms. To save time on solving the firm's problem repeatedly, I solve the firm's value function on an additional grid of θ's including 25% above and 25% below the steady state values. For conjectured θ's off the grid, I use linear interpolation on the policy functions. I then iterate on θ until the aggregated micro behavior of a panel of firms generates the conjectured θ, updating *theta* using a convex combination of the conjecture and the simulated tightness with a relatively low damping parameter.

B.1 Approximate Equilibrium Algorithm

The solution to the approximate aggregate equilibrium is as follows. As state above, I conjecture log-linear equations of motion for the aggregate "states":

$$\begin{aligned}
\ln \bar{L}' &= \gamma_{l0} + \gamma_{l1} \ln \bar{L} + \gamma_{l2} \ln \bar{N} + \gamma_{l3} \ln p \\
\ln \bar{N}' &= \gamma_{N0} + \gamma_{N1} \ln \bar{L} + \gamma_{N2} \ln \bar{N} + \gamma_{N3} \ln p \\
\ln \theta' &= \gamma_{\theta 0} + \gamma_{\theta 1} \ln \bar{L}' + \gamma_{\theta 2} \ln \bar{N}' + \gamma_{\theta 3} \ln p'
\end{aligned}$$

Again, the forecast equation for θ is used by the firm to form expectations of hiring costs today and in the future period. The task is to solve for the coefficients $\{\gamma_L, \gamma_N, \gamma_\theta\}$.

Implementing this procedure is computationally burdensome as it requires an additional four state variables for the firm's problem: $p, \bar{N}, \bar{L}, \theta$. It is important to discuss why θ must be a state variable for the firm. In principle, firms know the aggregate state of the economy and can therefore predict θ from $\bar{N}, \bar{L}, p$. However, forecast errors can lead to a situation in which the true market clearing level of θ is different from the forecasted level. Therefore, I forecast θ from the equation above but I solve the value function on a grid including 75% and 125% of that forecasted $\theta(\bar{N}, \bar{L})$. I use a coarse grid of 5 points in both $\bar{N}$ and $\bar{L}$ and three points for θ.

While the forecast equations ultimately are very accurate, it is not enough to use the forecasted aggregate variables $\bar{N}, \bar{L}, \theta$ as the equilibrium aggregate state at each stage of the simulation. Instead, in each period of the simulation, I iterate on $\bar{N}, \bar{L}, \theta$, using the firm's optimal policy for each guess of the aggregate state, until the micro behavior is consistent with the aggregate state.

In summary, the algorithm proceeds as follows:

1. Guess $\Pi^0(n, \ell, x, p, \{\bar{N}, \bar{L}, \theta\}; \gamma^{\mathbf{j}})$ and $\gamma^{\mathbf{j}}$

2. Solve for the value function, Π^j, and associated policy function, Φ^j

3. Simulate the model for 2000 periods and 10,000 agents per period starting each firm at the steady state level of the idiosyncratic states. I discard the first 200 periods.

4. In each period, t, of the simulation solve for the market clearing aggregate state. I start with last period's aggregate state as a guess. I iterate on $\{\bar{N}, \bar{L}, \theta\}$ until the aggregate micro behavior is consistent with the guessed state.

5. Run OLS regressions to obtain simulated γ_{OLS} coefficients. If the difference between the γ^j and γ_{OLS} is smaller than a pre-specified tolerance, stop.

6. Otherwise, set the conjecture for $\gamma^{j+1} = \lambda \gamma^j + (1-\lambda)\gamma_{\text{OLS}}$, $\lambda \in (0,1)$ and start at 1.

For the calibrated parameters, the equilibrium forecast equations are as follows:

$$\ln \bar{L}' = .0062 + .9724 \ln \bar{L} + .0167 \ln \bar{N} - .0823 \ln p, \ R^2 = .997 \tag{B.1}$$

$$\ln \bar{N}' = -.0315 + .0118 \ln \bar{L} + .8692 \ln \bar{N} + .1303 \ln p, \ R^2 = .971 \tag{B.2}$$

$$\ln \theta' = 3.2596 + .6804 \ln \bar{L}' + 15.4623 \ln \bar{N}' + 8.6422 \ln p', \ R^2 = .988 \tag{B.3}$$

The R^2 for this solution are in the same ballpark as those in Bils et al. (2011). It is worth mentioning that since I use a simple stochastic simulation with only 10,000 agents and 2,000 periods, the R^2 are low due to simulation error. Increasing the size of the panel and the length of the panel would increase the R^2 but with the lost of a large increase in computational time. I simulate aggregate data and impulse responses using the optimal decision policy of the firm as solved above.

B.2 Larger Stochastic Simulations

For the baseline results, I used a stochastic simulation size of 10,000 firms over 2,000 periods, discarding the first 200 observations for a burn-in period. Here, I show the results of solution to the baseline model with a larger panel of firms. I expand the number of firms from 10,000 to 30,000 while keeping the number of periods constant. The R^2 from these regressions are as follows. From the regression for $\ln L'$ it is .9973, for $\ln N'$ it is .9738, and for $\ln \theta'$ it is .9928. Just adding additional firms to the simulation increases the goodness of fit in each regression and most for the lower R^2 from the prediction for future labor market tightness. Additional agents would further increase the precision, but the results are quantitatively similar.

C Data Analysis with Missing States

Table A1 denotes states that I was restricted from accessing due to legal restrictions between the state and the BLS. The BLS provided a dataset of job flow statistics calculated at the establishment level for all states at the 2-digit NAICS level. With these data, I provide an additional robustness check to ensure that the missing states do not materially affect the econometric results.

The main difference between these data and the firm-level data is that job flows are calculated at the establishment level. In addition, they include opening and closing establishments in the job creation and job destruction measures. Nonetheless, the regressions in Table 6 provide a useful check on the empirical results. Table 6 shows that including the additional states does not change the main results that higher experience rating reduces both job destruction and job creation rates. With these data, I find that increasing the marginal tax cost to 100% would reduce job destruction by 12.7% and job creation by 13.3% (Table 6).

Figure 1: Typical Tax Schedule, Reserve Ratio

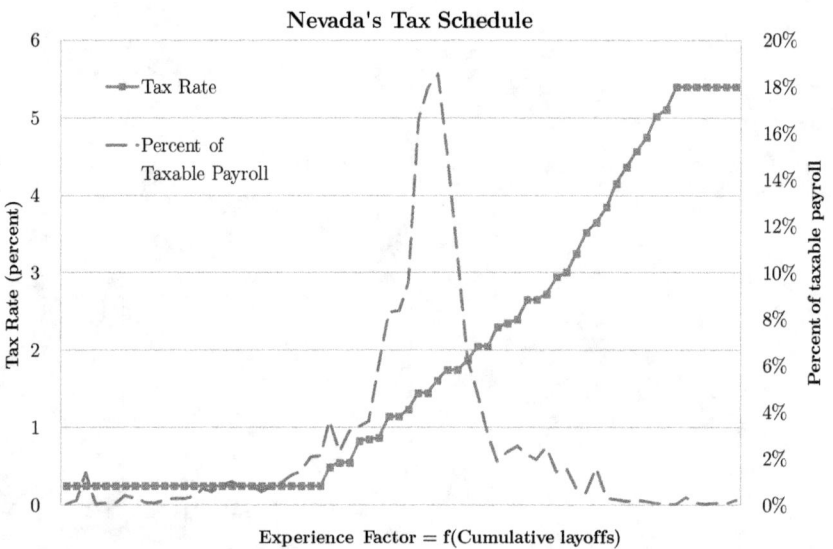

Figure 2: Typical Tax Schedule, Benefit Ratio

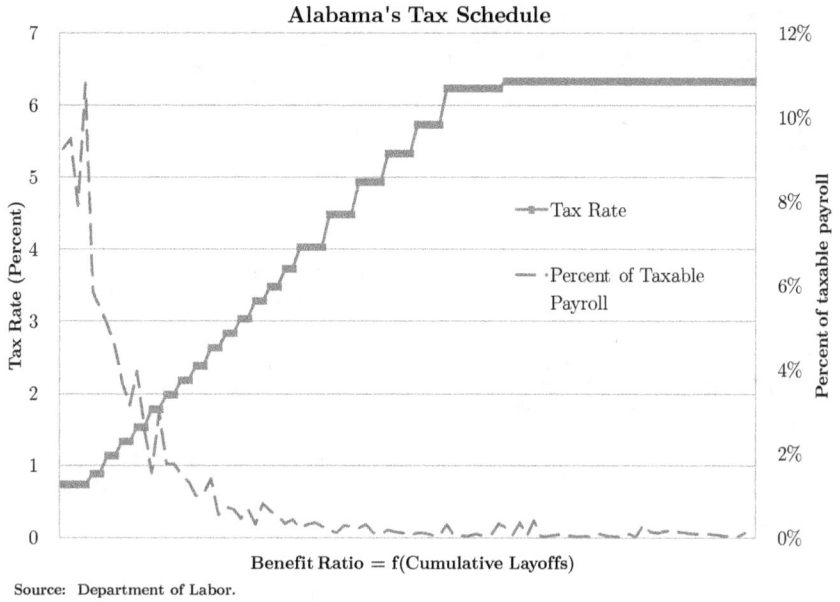

Figure 3: Parameterized Tax Schedule

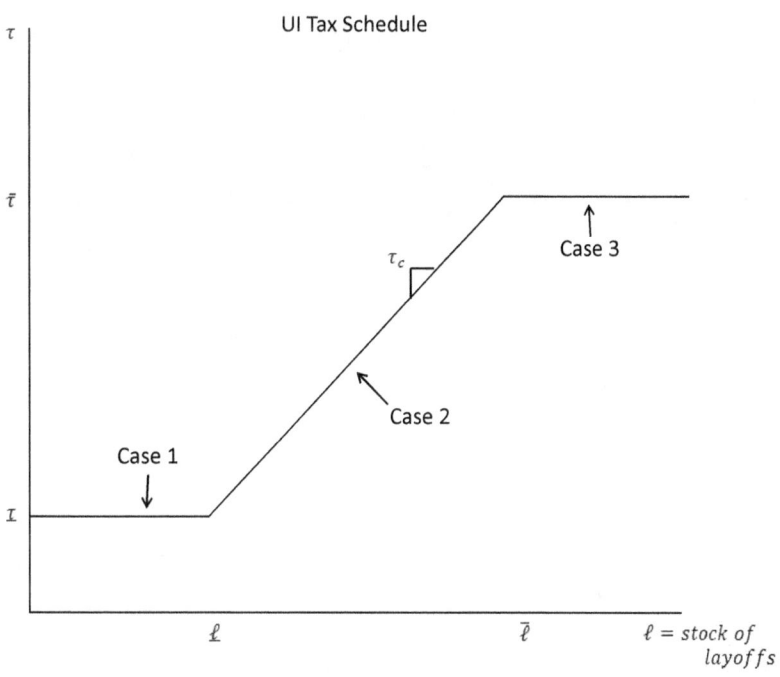

Figure 4a: Policy Function, Case 1

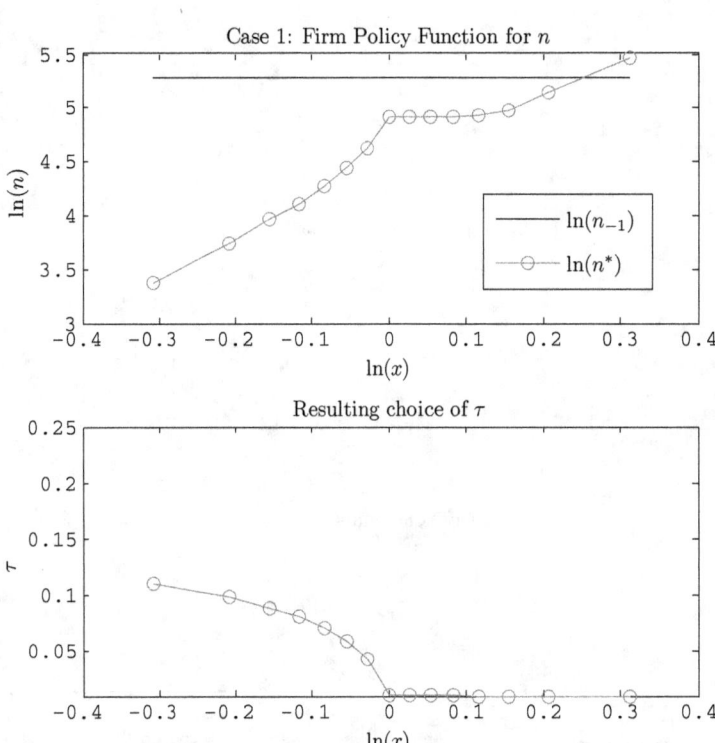

Figure 4b: Policy Function, Case 2

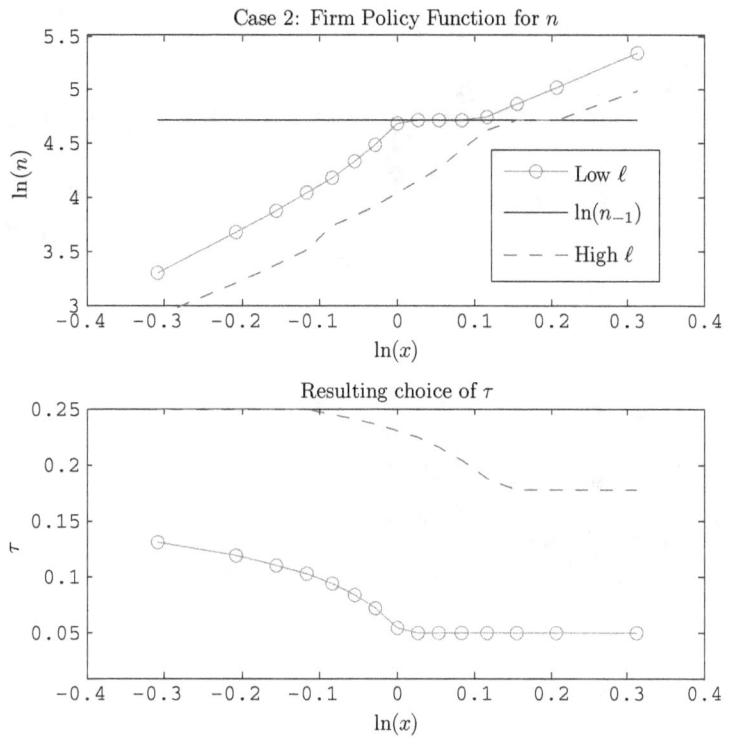

Figure 5: Experience Rating and Job Flows

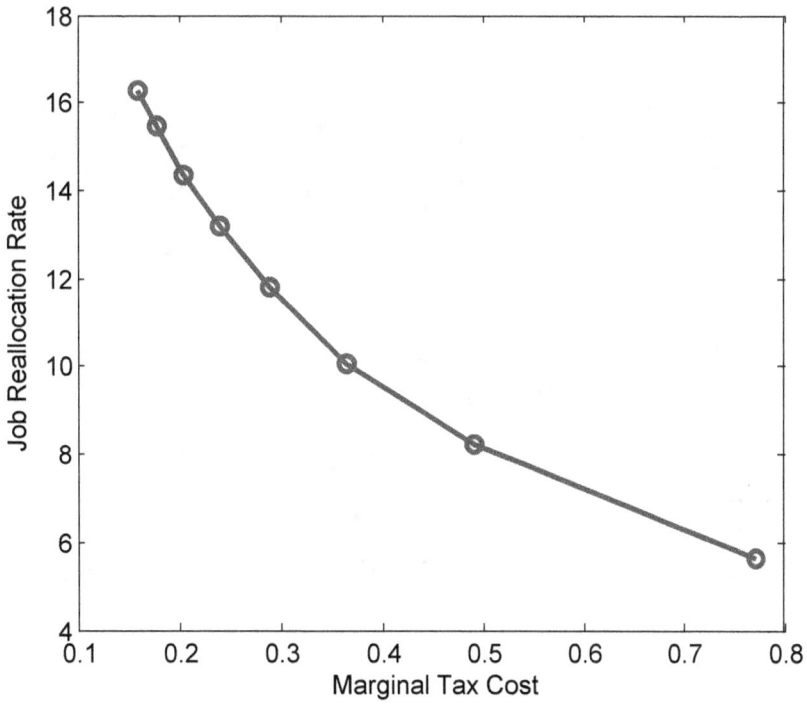

Figure 6: Distribution of Marginal Tax Costs

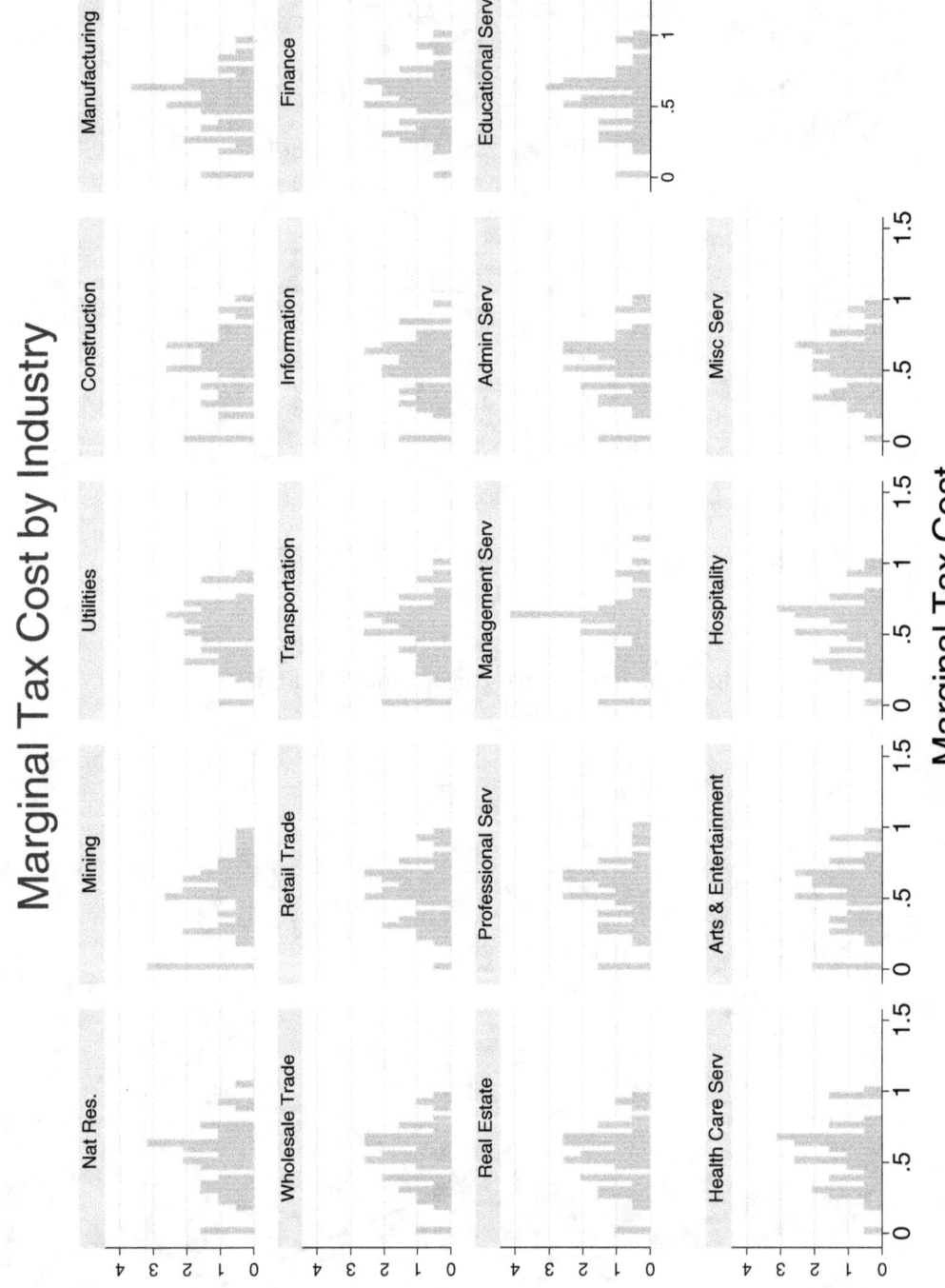

Author's analysis of QCEW data

Figure 7: Distribution of Taxes in Model

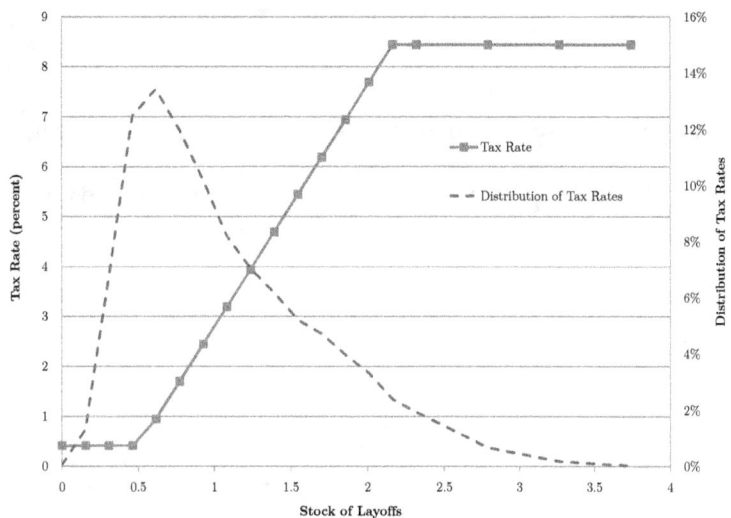

Figure 8: Types of Tax Changes

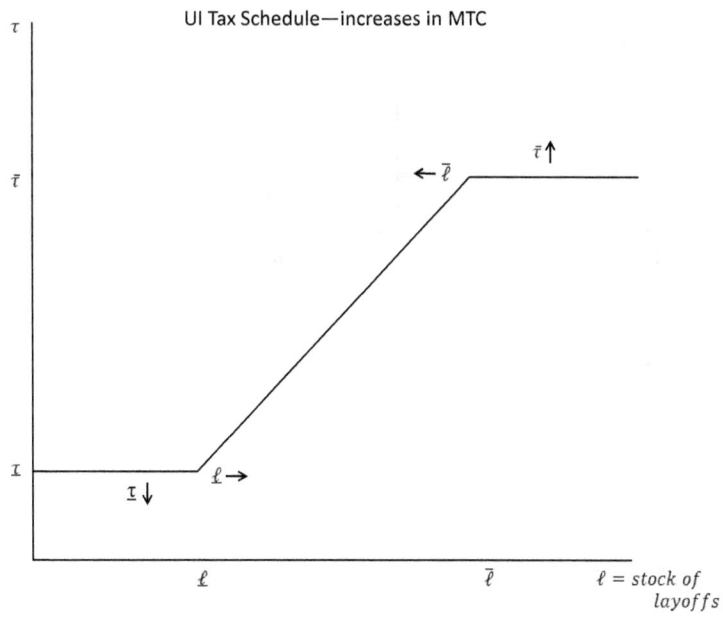

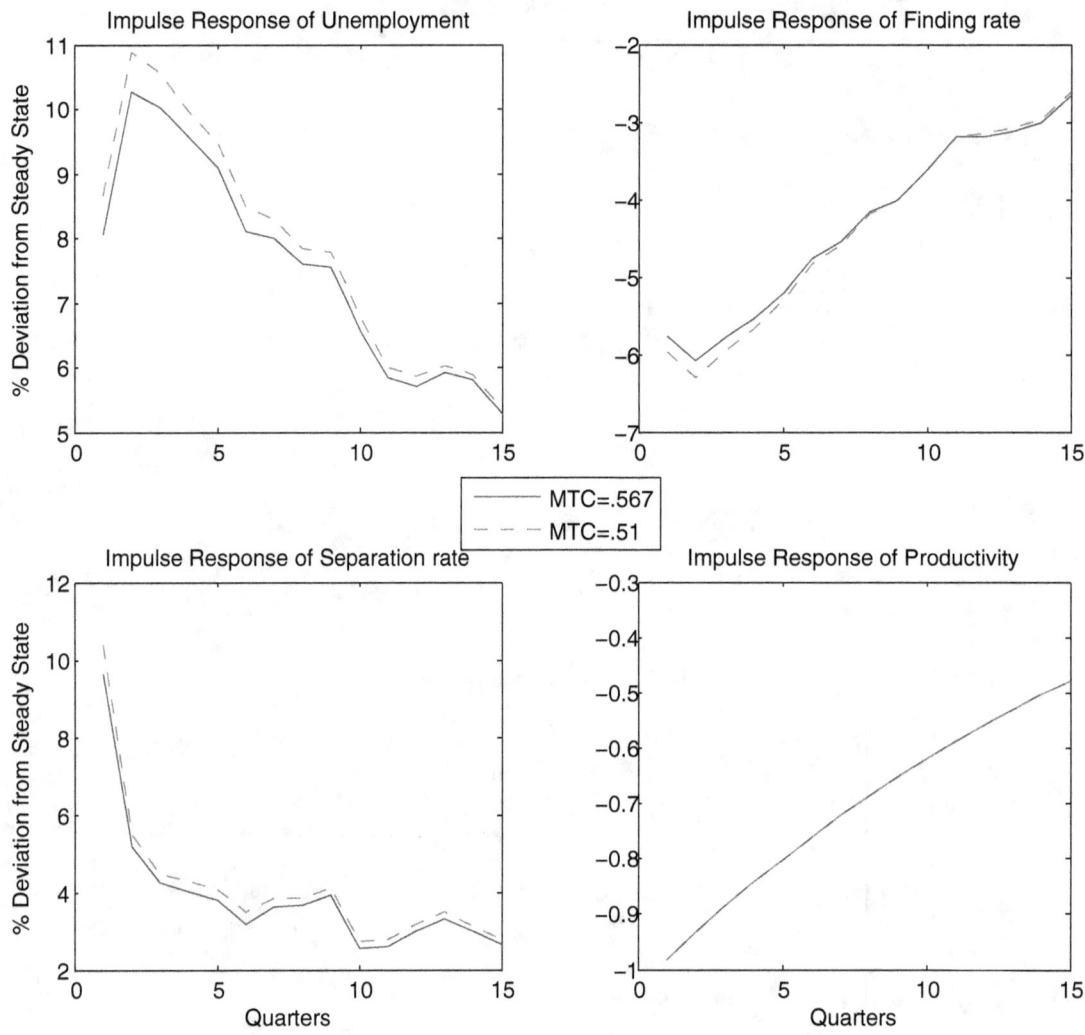

Figure 9: Impulse Response to Negative 1% Aggregate Shock

Figure 10: Nonlinear Response of Unemployment

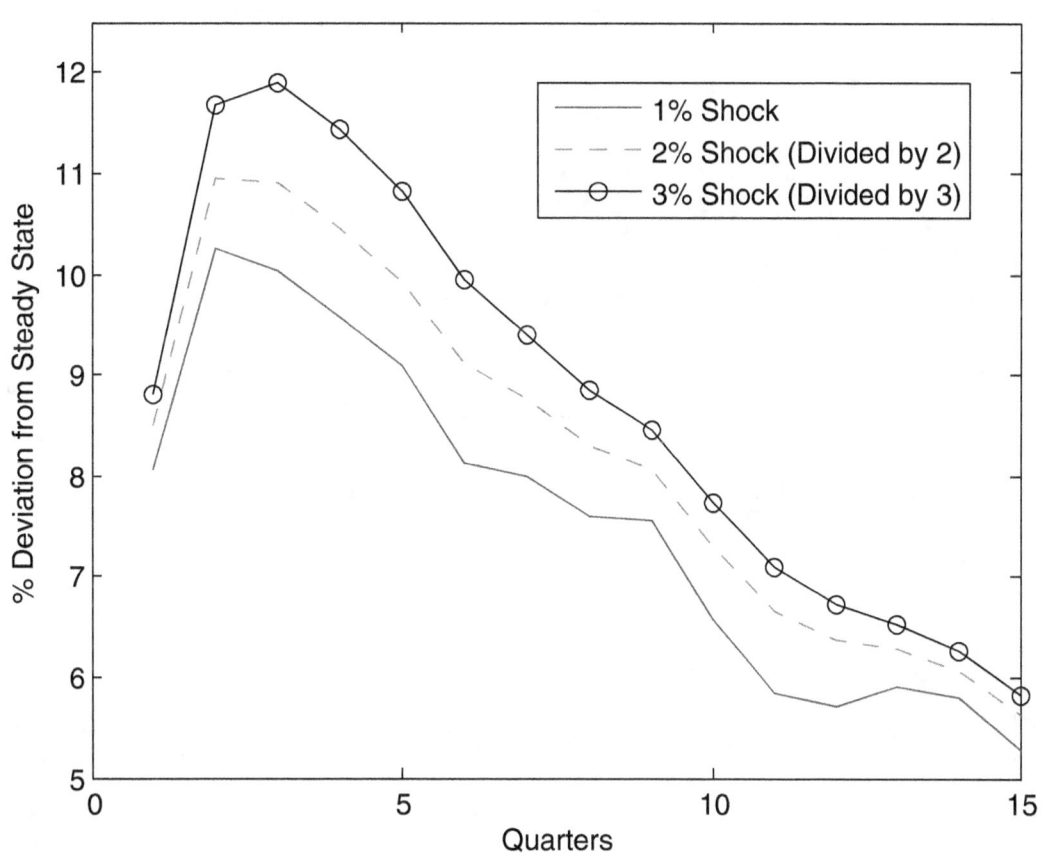

Figure 11: Impulse Response to Positive 1% Aggregate Shock

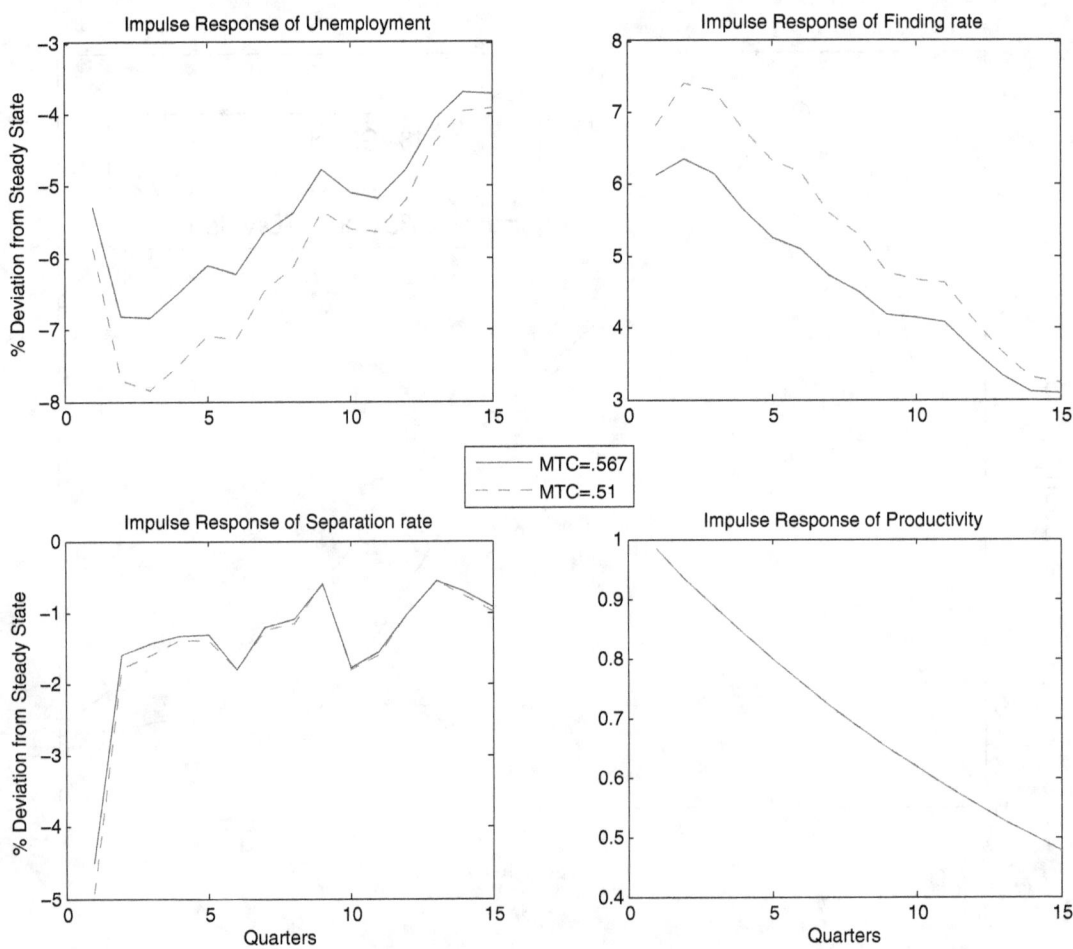

Figure 12: Nonlinear Response of Unemployment

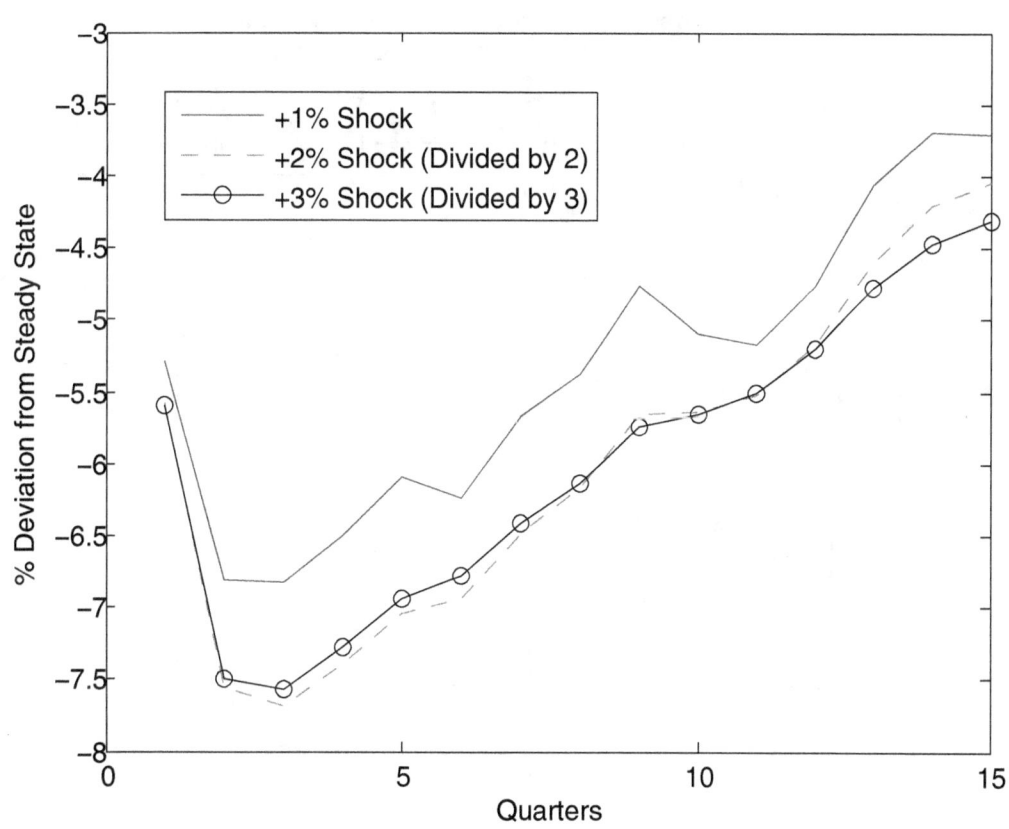

Figure 13: Tax Distributions

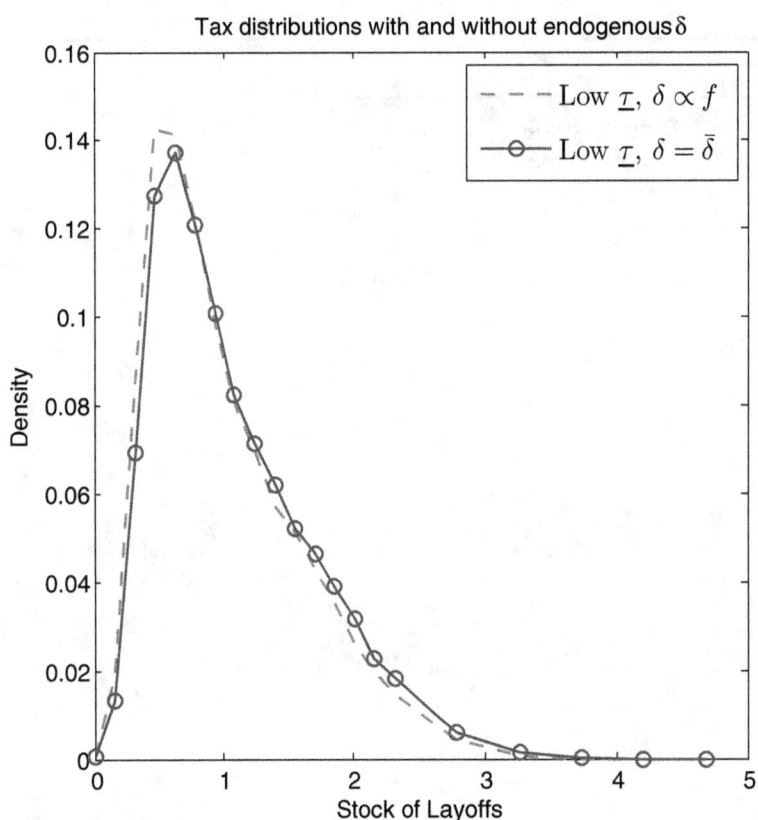

Figure 14: Impulse Response to Negative 1% Aggregate Shock, endogenous δ

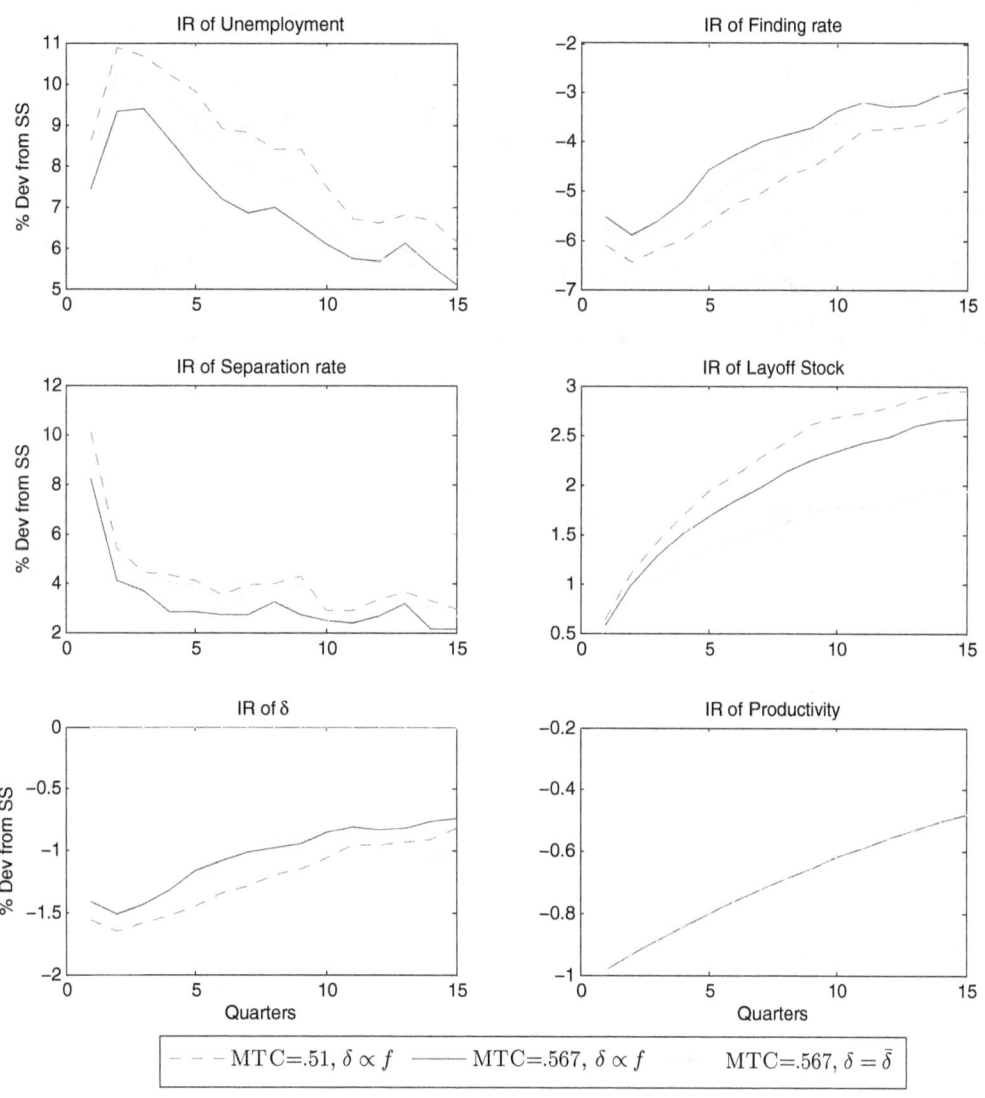

Table 1: Summary Statistics

	Mean	Std. Dev	Min	Max
Averaged MTC, i=.1, All Years	0.54	0.21	0.00	2.17
Average MTC, i=estimated, 2001-2010	0.61	0.22	0.00	2.20
Average MTC, i=.1, All Years. $g_n=0$	0.63	0.24	0.00	1.16
Average MTC, i=.1. All Years. Topel	0.62	0.23	0.00	1.09
Job Destruction	6.48	7.40	0.02	185.71
Job Creation	6.23	7.61	0.02	191.11
Net Creation Rate	-0.25	8.73	-176.71	175.85
Job Reallocation	12.49	9.92	0.17	182.27
Total Employment	21599	51694	1	1039293
Total Firms	1145	4785	1	274690
Number of 3-digit industry X state cells		3,377		
Number of 3-digit industry X state cells, 2001-2010		123,086		
Number of 3-digit industry X state cells, All Years		264,932		

Source: Author's analysis of QCEW data.

Table 2: Regression Analysis. Marginal Tax Cost and Job Flows

Dependent Variable	Regressor: Averaged MTC. i=.10 All Years			Regressor: Averaged MTC. i=.10 2001-2010		
	Coefficient	Mean LHS	Change from average MTC to 1	Coefficient	Mean LHS	Change from average MTC to 1
JD Rate	-2.4**	6.48	-17.0%	-3.05***	6.16	-22.7%
	(0.98)			(1.01)		
JC Rate	-1.86**	6.23	-13.7%	-1.73**	5.87	-15.6%
	(0.87)			(0.86)		
JR Rate	-2.69**	12.5	-10.0%	-3.27**	11.58	-13.0%
	(1.29)			(1.32)		
Net Creation Rate	.81**	-0.25		1.53***	-0.29	
	(0.25)			(0.34)		
N	264,932			101,301		

Author's analysis of QCEW data. Covariates: State, 3-digit NAICS, year, quarter fixed effects, total employment and total number of firms. Standard errors are clustered at the 3-digit industry X state cell. (*p<.10, **p<.05, ***p<.01)

Table 3: Regression Analysis. Marginal Tax Cost and Job Flows. Alternate Marginal Tax Costs

	Regressor: Averaged MTC. No g_n All Years			Regressor: Averaged Topel MTC. $i=.1$ All Years		
Dependent Variable	Coefficient	Mean LHS	Change from average MTC to 1	Coefficient	Mean LHS	Change from average MTC to 1
JD Rate	-2.76***	6.48	-15.8%	-2.29***	6.48	-13.4%
	(1.04)			(0.79)		
JC Rate	-2.59***	6.23	-15.4%	-2.71***	6.23	-16.5%
	(0.98)			(0.87)		
JR Rate	-3.36**	12.5	-9.9%	-3.94***	12.5	-11.9%
	(1.37)			(1.29)		
Net Creation Rate	.41	-0.25		-.44***	-0.25	
	(0.28)			(0.25)		
N	264,932			264,932		

Author's analysis of QCEW data. Covariates: State, 3-digit NAICS, year, quarter fixed effects, total employment and total number of firms. Standard errors are clustered at the 3-digit industry X state cell. (*p<.10, **p<.05,***p<.01)

Table 4: Regression Analysis. Marginal Tax Cost and Job Flows

Alternative Marginal Tax Costs II

	Regressor: Averaged MTC. $i=.05$ All Years			Regressor: Averaged MTC. $i=.15$ All Years			Regressor: Averaged MTC. i=estimated 2001-2010		
Dependent Variable	Coefficient	Mean LHS	Change from average MTC to 1	Coefficient	Mean LHS	Change from average MTC to 1	Coefficient	Mean LHS	Change from average MTC to 1
JD Rate	-2.19**	6.48	-12.2%	-2.65***	6.48	-21.7%	-4.5***	6.16	-28.5%
	(0.84)			(1.12)			0.84		
JC Rate	-1.79**	6.23	-10.3%	-1.93**	6.23	-16.4%	-3.4***	5.87	-22.6%
	(0.75)			(0.98)			0.78		
JR Rate	-3.36**	12.5	-9.7%	-2.85*	12.5	-12.1%	-6.1***	11.58	-20.50%
	(1.37)			(1.47)			(0.29)		
Net Creation Rate	.62***	-0.25		.965***	-0.25		1.18*	-0.29	
	(0.20)			(0.29)			(1.19)		
N	264,932			264,932			123,898		

Author's analysis of QCEW data. Covariates: State, 3-digit NAICS, year, quarter fixed effects, total employment and total number of firms. Standard errors are clustered at the 3-digit industry X state cell. (*p<.10, **p<.05,***p<.01)

Table 5: Regression Analysis. Marginal Tax Cost and Job Flows. Additional covariates

	Dependent Variable: JD Rate			Dependent Variable: JC Rate		
	(1)	(2)		(1)	(2)
Averaged MTC i=.1	1.34	-3.31***	Averaged MTC i=.1	2.82***	-1.23***
	(1.07)	(0.33)		(0.99)	(0.29)
Proportion on slope	1.94**	0.67	Proportion on slope	3.4***	1.01***
	(0.78)	(0.26)		(0.76)	(0.25)
Prop Slope*MTC	-3.31**		Prop Slope*MTC	-5.1***	
	(1.39)			(1.30)	
% Benefits Charged		-0.36	% Benefits Charged		-0.63
		(0.50)			(0.47)
Minimum Rate		0.12	Minimum Rate		0.04
		(0.09)			(0.09)
Maximum Rate		.05*	Maximum Rate		0.04
		(0.03)			(0.03)
Years	2001-2010	2001-2010	Years	2001-2010	2001-2010
N	103,306	101,011	N	103,244	100,955

Author's analysis of QCEW data. Covariates: State, 3-digit NAICS, year, quarter fixed effects, total employment and total number of firms. Standard errors are clustered at the 3-digit industry X state cell (*p<.10, **p<.05,***p<.01)

Table 6: Regression Analysis. Marginal Tax Cost and Job Flows

Two Digit Data with Excluded States

	Regressor: Averaged MTC. i=.10		
	1992 Q2-2010 Q1		
Dependent Variable	Coefficient	Mean LHS	Change from average MTC to 1
JD Rate	-2.12**	7.95	-12.7%
	(0.85)		
JC Rate	-2.27***	8.13	-13.3%
	(0.86)		
JR Rate	-4.39***	16	-13.0%
	(1.68)		
Net Creation Rate	-.15	0.18	
	(0.27)		
Clusters	891		
N	98,010		

Author's analysis of QCEW data. Covariates: State, 2-digit NAICS, year, quarter fixed effects, total employment and total number of firms. Standard errors are clustered at the 2-digit industry X state cell. (*p<.10, **p<.05,***p<.01)

Table 7: Regression Analysis. Marginal Tax Cost and Job Flows

Single Establishment Firms Only

	Regressor: Averaged MTC. i=.10 1992 Q2-2010 Q1		
Dependent Variable	Coefficient	Mean LHS	Change from average MTC to 1
JD Rate	-2.16**	7.06	-14.0%
	(0.95)		
JC Rate	-1.58*	7.30	-10.0%
	(0.86)		
Clusters	3377		
N	264,094		

Author's analysis of QCEW data. Covariates: State, 3-digit NAICS, year, quarter fixed effects, total employment and total number of firms. Standard errors are clustered at the 3-digit industry X state cell (*p<.10, **p<.05,***p<.01)

Table 8: Regression Analysis. Marginal Tax Cost and Extry/Exit

	Regressor: Averaged MTC All Years	
Dependent Variable	Coefficient	Mean LHS
Birth Rate	-.15	2.20%
	(0.25)	
Death Rate	-.06	3.40%
	(0.20)	
Clusters	3347	
N	218,836	

Author's analysis of QCEW data. Covariates: State, 3-digit NAICS, year, quarter fixed effects, total employment and total number of firms. Standard errors are clustered at the 3-digit industry X state cell. (*p<.10, **p<.05,***p<.01)

Table 9: Calibrated Parameters

	Parameter	Meaning	Value	Reason
	β	Discount factor	.996	Annual interest rate of 5%
	α	Scale parameter	.59	Labor's share $\approx$ .72
	η	Bargaining power	.4	
See Section 5.5 "External"	ϕ	Matching elasticity	.6	Petrongolo & Pissarides (2001)
	p	Steady state productivity	1	Normalization
	ρ_p	Persistence of p	.983	Persistence of ALP .95 quarterly
	σ^p	Std. dev. of ϵ^p	.005	$\sigma(APL) = .02$
	$\mathbb{L}$	Labor force	.8553	Tightness= .72
	μ	Matching efficiency	.5132	Finding rate= .45
	$\underline{\tau}$	Minimum tax rate	.417%	Average minimum tax rate in data
	$\overline{\tau}$	Maximum tax rate	8.44%	Average maximum tax rate in data
"Internal"	b	Leisure value	.7934	Sep. rate=3.1%
	c	Flow cost vacancy	.2828	Hiring cost= 14% quarterly wage
	ρ_x	Persistence of x	.9504	$P(|\%\Delta n| < .05) = 54.5\%$
	σ^x	Std. dev. of ϵ^x	.1721	$JR = 12.5\%$
	δ	Depreciation of layoffs	.026	$P(\tau = \underline{\tau}) = 17.7, P(\tau = \overline{\tau}) = 6.6\%$
	$\underline{\ell}$	Lower tax threshold	.5085	$MTC = 54\%$
	$\overline{\ell}$	Upper tax threshold	2.16	

Table 10: Calibrated Targets and Moments

Moment	Symbol	Target	Value
Separation Rate (b)	s	3.1%	3.53%
Hiring Cost (c)	$\frac{c/q}{w_q}$	14%	14.74%
Non-adjustment Prob. (ρ_x)	$P(|\%\Delta n| < .05)$	54.5%	45%
Job reallocation (σ^x)	JR	12.5%	7.05%
Tightness ($\mathbb{L}$)	θ_{ss}	.72	.72
Finding Rate (μ)	f_{ss}	45%	45%
Minimum Rate ($\underline{\ell}$)	$P(\tau = \underline{\tau})$	17.7%	17.43%
Maximum Rate ($\overline{\ell}$)	$P(\tau = \overline{\tau})$	6.6%	6.76%
Marginal Tax Cost (δ)	MTC	54%	53.7%

Table 11: Steady State Tax Experiments. Percentage changes unless noted

Change in:	Param	MTC	JC,JD	Revenue	Π	u % pts.	%Δu
→$\underline{\ell}$	15.5%	5%	-1.1%	-8.6%	.06%	-.31	-4.3%
←$\bar{\ell}$	-3.7%	5%	-1.1%	2.3%	-.38%	-.02	-.28%
↓$\underline{\tau}$	-.2% pts	5%	-1.9%	-8.6%	.07%	-.33	-4.5%
↑$\bar{\tau}$	.4% pts	5%	-1.5%	2.3%	-.26%	-.18	-2.5%
Steady State		54%	3.53%	.022	76.65	7.27%	

Table 12: Closing 50% of Net Reserve Gap. Percentage changes unless noted

Change in:	Param	MTC	JC,JD	Revenue	Π	u % pts.	%Δu
↑$\underline{\tau}$,↑$\bar{\tau}$	+.2%,+.2%	0%	.85%	9.1%	-.29%	.11	1.5%
←$\bar{\ell}$	-12.4%	-19.4%	-1.1%	9.1%	-.6%	-.13	-1.8%
Steady State		54%	3.53%	.022	76.65	7.27%	

Table 13: Steady State Tax Experiments, $\delta \propto f$. Percentage changes unless noted

Change in:	Param	MTC	JC,JD	Revenue	Π	u % pts.	%Δu
→$\underline{\ell}$	15.50%	5%	-1.42%	-10.45%	0.06%	-0.37%	-5.1%
←$\bar{\ell}$	-3.70%	5%	-0.57%	2.27%	-0.15%	-0.02%	-0.28%
↓$\underline{\tau}$	-.2% pts	5%	-2.27%	-10.00%	0.07%	-5.09%	-0.37%
↑$\bar{\tau}$	.40% pts	5%	-1.42%	1.36%	-0.25%	-0.17%	-2.34%
Steady State		54%	3.53%	.022	76.65	7.27%	

Table A.1: List of States

State	States Excluded from QCEW. Included in Table 6	State	States Excluded from QCEW. Included in Table 6
Reserve Ratio		Benefit Ratio	
Arkansas		Alabama	
Arizona		Connecticut	
California		Florida	X
Colorado		Iowa	
DC		Illinois	X
Georgia		Maryland	
Hawaii		Minnesota	
Idaho		Mississippi	X
Indiana		Oregon	X
Kansas		Texas	
Kentucky		Utah	
Louisiana		Virginia	
Massachusetts	X	Vermont	
Maine		Washington	
Missouri		Wyoming	X
Montana			
North Carolina			
North Dakota			
Nebraska			
New Hampshire	X		
New Jersey			
New Mexico			
Nevada			
New York	X		
Ohio			
Puerto Rico			
Rhode Island			
South Carolina			
South Dakota			
Tennessee			
Wisconsin	X		
West Virginia			
Number of Reserve Ratio States: 32		Number of Benefit Ratio States: 15	

Note: Author's analysis of DOL and QCEW data. States with an "X" were excluded in Tables 1-5 due to restrictions in QCEW data. Table 6 includes these states using analysis of 2-digit aggregated data of the QCEW provided by the BLS.